SHELTERING TREES

THE POWER, PROMISE, AND REFUGE OF
friendship

DONNA VANLIERE
& EDDIE CARSWELL OF NEWSONG

HOWARD
PUBLISHING CO.

Our purpose at Howard Publishing is to:

- *Increase faith* in the hearts of growing Christians
- *Inspire holiness* in the lives of believers
- *Instill hope* in the hearts of struggling people everywhere

Because He's coming again!

Sheltering Trees: The Power, Promise, and Refuge of Friendship
© 2001 by Donna VanLiere
All rights reserved. Printed in the United States of America
Published by Howard Publishing Co., Inc.
3117 North 7th Street, West Monroe, Louisiana 71291-2227

01 02 03 04 05 06 07 08 09 10   10 9 8 7 6 5 4 3 2 1

Edited by Philis Boultinghouse
Interior design by Lecy Design, Minneapolis, Minnesota

Library of Congress Cataloging-in-Publication Data
VanLiere, Donna, 1966–
     Sheltering trees : the power, promise, and refuge of friendship / Donna
VanLiere & Eddie Carswell.
        p. cm.
     ISBN 1-58229-170-5
        1. Friendship—Religious aspects—Christianity. I. Carswell, Eddie. II. Title.

BV4647.F7 V36 2001
241'.6762—dc21   2001024139

Scripture quotations are taken from the Holy Bible, New Living Translation,
copyright © 1996. Used by permission of Tyndale House Publishers, Inc.,
Wheaton, Illinois 60189. All rights reserved.

To my special friend

_____

(From)

_____

(Date)

Friendship is a sheltering tree;

O! the joys, that came down shower-like,

Of Friendship, Love, and Liberty

FROM THE POEM "YOUTH AND AGE"
BY SAMUEL TAYLOR COLERIDGE (1772–1834)

CONTENTS

FOREWORD
by Eddie Carswell

$\mathcal{E}$nglish poet Samuel Coleridge said a friend is like a mighty sheltering tree. Sheltering trees are special people God puts into each of our lives; they stand strong beside us, covering us with prayer, no matter the circumstance.

The concept of sheltering trees came alive to me recently when a well-known Christian was struggling with his walk with the Lord. In speaking with a friend on the phone, we talked about this brother's falling and how people were reacting to it. While many felt the need to distance themselves from him, there were a few sheltering trees (those special friends!) whom God placed in his life to be ready for just such a time.

As a result of that situation, God allowed Leonard Alhstrom and me to write "Sheltering Tree," what we hope is a timely song about friendship. We were honored to have our friends and Christian music artists Mac Powell from Third Day, Rebecca St. James, Charlie Peacock, Carolyn Arends, Fred Hammond, and Natalie Grant to lend their voices to make powerful special guest appearances.

Now we have this wonderful book, written and compiled by Donna VanLiere. Donna is a godly woman and an insightful writer. In the pages of this book, you will read compelling stories of friendship based on her personal interviews with prominent music artists, authors, and speakers whose lives have been touched by special friends. From the heartwarming story of Randy Travis and a young friend he met through the Make-A-Wish Foundation to the powerful story of a praying friend in Stormie Omartian's life, this book will encourage and challenge you to appreciate your friendships and strive to be that sheltering friend God has appointed you to be in someone else's life.

Sheltering trees come in all sizes and shapes and sometimes from the most unlikely places. My father-in-law, Shell E. Hartley, was one of those special friends God placed in my life. Not too sure of me at first (I don't blame him, now that I have daughters of my own), we eventually became great buddies. A man of profound insight and discernment, he had a great sense of humor and was a wonderful poet; and he loved me even though I stole his baby daughter! He passed away last year, and I really miss him. He was a great sheltering tree in my life, and to him I dedicate my contribution to this book. It is my hope that you, too, will find and be such a friend.

We all need sheltering trees!

INTRODUCTION
by Donna VanLiere

While driving through Nashville on a brilliant spring afternoon, I stopped at a busy intersection where I noticed two young women sitting together at a bus stop. One was tall, her large frame amply carrying a great mass of weight, while the other was petite and svelte. By appearance alone, you would easily think they were strangers just waiting for the bus. However, as I sat watching them I noticed they were engaged in a carefree conversation. It wasn't guarded or stifled as it is with strangers or purposely polite as it can be with acquaintances. One filed her nails as the other dug through her purse looking for that last piece of lint-covered gum at the bottom of it, their conversation never waning for a moment. Glancing down the street and then to their watches, the decision was made to forsake the bus ride and walk to wherever they were headed. As they got up from the bench their disparate sizes could be seen in full view. These two really didn't *look* like friends. But as they began to walk, one of them said something that stopped the other in her tracks, doubling her over in laughter. The laughter shook her every inch, and she grabbed the shoulder of her friend in support; and together the two stood on the side of a busy street in Nashville and laughed in complete and total hysterics. There was no doubt that these two were *friends*.

Driving away I was reminded that a friend doesn't have a particular size or face, skin color or age, position or wealth. There are no rules or demands, conditions or limitations—friends are simply people who choose to open their lives to someone else, sharing joys and burdens, hardships and triumphs—not because they have to, but because they want to.

Within this book are stories of people who have chosen to be a friend and who have joyously celebrated the priceless treasure that is friendship. Their stories will touch, encourage, challenge, and most importantly, inspire your heart to spring up as a sheltering tree, providing power, promise, and refuge to someone who shares an undeniable, unmistakable connection to your soul—a friend.

Editor's Note: All stories (with the exception of the Arthur Ashe story) are based on interviews conducted by Donna VanLiere.

WE ALL NEED

SHELTERING TREES

FRIENDS IN OUR LIVES

friendship

We all need sheltering trees

Friends in our lives

who'll get down on their knees

And lift us up before

the King of Kings

We all need sheltering trees

RANDY TRAVIS &
KATIE BETH WATSON

*R*andy Travis has been a mainstay in country music for fifteen years. Number one hits like "Forever and Ever Amen," "I Told You So," and "Diggin' Up Bones" have rocketed record sales into the stratosphere. With more than twenty-five million records sold, Randy Travis is not only a mainstay but a country music superstar. But this country music icon doesn't have the "better-than-you" attitude or ego that so often accompanies a bona fide superstar. Gold and platinum records, awards and world travels have not affected the modest, self-effacing Marshville, North Carolina, native. "Places become a blur after fifteen years," he says in a rich baritone drawl. "You may forget years or places, but you can't forget a person who touches you."

Katie Beth Watson was a starry-eyed nine-year-old when her young life touched the singer's. "I was struck by how grown up she acted," he fondly remembers. "She was a very sweet little girl, but it wasn't like talking to a kid; it was more like talking to an adult." The Make-A-Wish Foundation had contacted Randy's management company with a request from a little girl who desperately wanted to meet the man behind the voice on so many of her favorite records. Katie had already undergone a heart transplant when Randy spent time with the lively, charming, brown-haired little girl backstage before one of his concerts. "I remember thinking that she looked like a normal child. You'd never think she'd had a heart transplant because she didn't look sick. She had bright eyes and rosy cheeks, and she loved to laugh. The only difference between her and any other child her age was how she spoke, but I guess you learn how to speak on an adult level very young in life when you go through something like that."

The Katie Beth whom Randy met that day was a sharp contrast to the picture Randy had seen. After her transplant Katie Beth was hooked to a complicated tangle of tubes, wires, and medical apparatus to help sustain her fragile life. "It was unbelievable how many wires and things were attached to her little body." As Randy sat talking with Katie Beth and her family, he was struck by how loving and kind each of them was. "Her folks were great with her," he recalls in a voice that reflects genuine warmth and respect. "They spent every minute they could with her, and they made every minute count. It made me aware of how I spend my own time with people I care about."

As the years progressed, it became obvious that the heart transplant was not working as doctors had hoped and that Katie Beth would have to endure another long operation. Since their first meeting, Randy had visited with the little girl several times but had never noticed a dramatic decline in her health. "She was always the same, sweet Katie Beth. If nobody had told me, I wouldn't have known that she was getting sicker." Before one of his concerts, Randy spent some uninterrupted time with Katie Beth and asked her

YOU MAY FORGET YEARS OR PLACES, BUT YOU CAN'T FORGET A PERSON WHO TOUCHES YOU.

RANDY TRAVIS

point-blank if she was going to have another transplant. "I'll never forget what she said to me," he says in deep awe. "She just looked at me and said, 'No, I don't want to go through that again. I know where I'm going when I die.'" The man who had made his living performing before millions of fans world-wide was humbled by the words of a sick little girl. "I was at a total loss for words," he recalls. "I couldn't say anything. I was amazed at her strength—how brave she was. Death wasn't something she was afraid of. She knew exactly where she was going, and she wasn't worried about it. I'd never seen such strength before."

One fall, Katie Beth made a trip to Salt Lake City, Utah, to watch Randy tape an episode of *Touched by an Angel*. It would be the last time he would see his little friend. "I could see she didn't feel well," he recalls, "but she was laughing and giggling just like she always did. She had a wonderful sense of humor." Katie Beth watched the taping process in amazement. After each take she sat wide-eyed as makeup and hair people swarmed Randy, powdering and pampering before the cameras rolled again. "Finally she said, 'I don't know how you can *stand* all that,'" he laughs. "She really was a funny little girl. I was so glad she was able to be there because she really enjoyed herself. She met Della Reese and Roma Downey and the other cast members. It was just great to have her there."

Shortly after the trip to Salt Lake City, Randy received word that Katie Beth had died. Thinking about his relationship with her, he realized that their friendship had made a tremendous impression on his life. "Our friendship did a lot more for *me* than it did for her. When you meet someone like Katie Beth, it makes you consider what you do in your life. That's what got to me more than anything else—how do I live my life? If you live how a godly person should, you can face death and anything else in life with Katie's kind of strength."

Randy spent more time with Katie Beth than any other child he's met in his fifteen-year career. "It's a good feeling to meet and talk with someone who wanted to meet you," he says warmly. "I love kids. I love to spend time with them and talk with them, and it's wonderful to be put in a place where people, especially kids who've maybe come out of a background of abuse or pain or sickness, want to talk and spend time with you. When you know that you've made them feel good just because you took the time to be a friend to them, to talk with them and get to know them—you think, *Well, maybe I've done a little bit of good in all I've been given in life.*"

RANDY TRAVIS & KATIE BETH WATSON

The years and places have continued to blur for Randy since Katie Beth's death, but the memory of the little child who looked death bravely in the face is still clear in his memory. "Her only problem was she was born with a weak heart," he says slowly, "but that never diminished her strength. She was a strong, brave, wonderful little girl and someone I'll remember for the rest of my life."

15

Randy recently released his fifteenth album, Inspirational Journey, *a labor of love that took four years to complete. He continues to work with the Make-A-Wish Foundation and others like it, considering it an honor to meet and talk with children just like Katie Beth across the nation.*

No love, no friendship

can cross the path of our destiny

without leaving some mark

on it forever.

FRANÇOIS MAURIAC

REBECCA ST. JAMES
KARLEEN LINDSEY

*D*ifferent seasons offer us a variety of life's friends along our journey. Some are there to inspire or encourage. Some are there to make us laugh or create priceless memories, while others are there to challenge or simply teach a lesson. Regardless of why they were in our lives or how long they were part of it, some friends will always remain unforgettable for the ineradicable effect they have on us.

At the age of fourteen, contemporary Christian music artist Rebecca St. James felt as if she didn't have a friend in the world—at least on this *side* of the world. Australian born, Rebecca found herself living on a brand-new continent, half a world away from her friends. "I was so lonely," she recalls. "I was being home-schooled, so I wasn't around other kids my age. I'd go to youth group, but everyone already had friends of their own. No one knew me; I was a foreigner. I'd go home crying because I didn't feel like I had any friends."

Wanting the pain of loneliness to go away, Rebecca began to pray that God would bring a strong, Christian friend into her life—"Someone who would encourage and challenge me in my faith, someone to go deep into God with." Months later Rebecca noticed a new face in the youth group. A leader promptly introduced the two "newcomers." "I didn't think she'd like me as a friend," Rebecca says. Laughing, she adds, "She looked like a cheerleader!" But Rebecca knew what it was like to be new and lonely, and her heart reached out to befriend the sad-looking girl.

The girls immediately clicked. Karleen Lindsey was the friend Rebecca had prayed for! "She's not the type of friend you feel labored to be around," states Rebecca. "She's encouraging and consistent. She's a strengthening friend; she built me up." In her charming Australian accent she giggles, "And I love her sense of humor. She makes me laugh. She can be ditzy in the most adorable way."

> YOU NEED SOMEONE TO SHARE THEIR LIFE AND WISDOM, SUCCESSES AND FAILURES WITH YOU, AND NO ONE DOES THAT QUITE LIKE A FRIEND.
>
> REBECCA ST. JAMES

Rebecca desperately needed the encouragement of her friend before a concert in Nashville. "Nashville is so nerve-racking," Rebecca unequivocally states. "It's the hometown show. Lots of music people there. I was very nervous." Sensing her friend's anxieties, Karleen took her hand, looked her in the eye and said, "Rebecca, remember it's all for God. All for God."

"The beautiful thing about her is that she doesn't care about my music," says Rebecca. "She's grateful for my ministry, but our friendship is based on something so much deeper—she likes me for Rebecca, not my music. She's *so* the real thing!"

Karleen fell in love and married at eighteen with Rebecca standing at her side as the proud maid of honor. Karleen experienced joys of motherhood a little more than a year later. "Our lives have gone in *totally* different directions," Rebecca states. "She actually has two children now, but we can *still* relate to each other. God is teaching us the same things, but we're learning them in different ways. As we talk about the deep issues of life, we grow together—that's true friendship. That's Karleen."

In an earlier season of life, Rebecca was involved with Girls Brigade in Sydney. At one particular meeting, the visiting pastor talked to the girls about giving their lives to God. "I knew it was something I wanted to do because I loved God, but I was nervous about it." As the pastor finished his comments, eight-year-old Lucy Prior leaned over and encouraged her reluctant friend to take the step forward. "I know God used her to encourage me," Rebecca states emphatically. "It always reminds me of the power a friend has." Laughing, she adds, "For an eight-year-old to challenge another eight-year-old is pretty significant!"

Rebecca has lost track of her friend from so many years ago, but Lucy's never strayed too far from her mind. "I'm able to do altar calls in my concerts, and whenever I see a little girl about that age come forward, I get very emotional. If I could see Lucy now, I would thank her for having the courage in that moment to challenge me, to encourage me to take that step."

At times Rebecca wonders if she herself could have been more encouraging or challenging to friends who have passed through her life. Around the time she met Karleen, Rebecca met another young girl in youth group. Her parents were divorced, and the young girl often seemed terribly sad and hurt. At youth camp she confided in Rebecca that she missed her father and longed for a man in her life. "She ached for that love," Rebecca recalls. At graduation the girl went off to college with dreams of becoming a doctor, and the two youth-group chums lost track of each other.

A couple of years later, Rebecca ran into the young woman at a local supermarket. "We chatted and made small talk," she remembers, "but I could see a deadness in her eyes. There was a sadness there." Her friend confided that she was pregnant and alone. "It was tearing her up inside," Rebecca says quietly. "It was a tremendous hurt. She gave away something very special and would be having a baby with no father in the picture."

KARLEEN LINDSEY & REBECCA ST. JAMES

This poignant meeting was a wake-up call for Rebecca. "Seeing her made me more passionate about telling girls that living a pure life is the best way. I've seen the hurt and pain in my friend's life. I've seen the effects of what not waiting can do."

Thoughts of various friends she's met on her journey prompted Rebecca to write a song in 1998 about keeping God as the third cord that binds friendship together called "I'll Carry You." "Keep God at the center of your friendship," Rebecca states simply. "That makes for the deepest level of friendship possible."

In February 2000, Rebecca won her first Grammy Award for Best Rock Gospel Album of the Year. She recently released her fifth studio album.

A true friend is somebody

who can make us do

what we can.

RALPH WALDO EMERSON

It's been said a friend is like

a mighty sheltering tree

A place of refuge we can run

when trouble comes for you and me

A FRIEND
IS LIKE

A SHELTERING
TREE

A PLACE OF REFUGE

friendship

LUCI SWINDOLL
MARILYN MEBERG

Convincingly, laughter was created for the good of the human body and spirit. A snicker can be triggered somewhere deep within, and in seconds it can permeate every inch of our bodies, fully manifesting itself in an all-out belly laugh. At that very moment stresses are relieved, anxieties are reduced, and ulcers take a break. Laughter is never as rich, never as fulfilling as when it is shared with friends. There is tremendous freedom in throwing our heads back, doubling over, and pounding the table in absolute and complete abandon.

Luci Swindoll and Marilyn Meberg discovered the joys and benefits of laughing together nearly thirty years ago. "Our friendship is built on sharing a love for books, art, the theater, deep conversations, and a zany, wacky humor," says Marilyn. "Luci is unpredictably funny and delightfully wacky!"

The two met when Luci was visiting her brother, Dr. Charles Swindoll, in Fullerton, California. Charles Swindoll had months earlier told Marilyn that she reminded him of his sister. When they finally met, there was an immediate connection. "There was an instant sense of kinship," Marilyn states.

At the time, Luci lived and worked in Dallas for Mobil Oil Corporation. A few months later she was transferred to the Fullerton area, and her friendship with Marilyn began to grow and flourish. "I discovered that Marilyn is an excellent listener, almost without parallel," Luci recalls. "She listens carefully and attentively, which is a lost art. I enjoyed my conversations with her, and I instantly connected with her sense of humor. She's a bit on the fringe of the absurd…a few bubbles off plum, and I love that!"

Keeping their friendship on the fringe of the absurd has proven to be a challenge and an extraordinary source of enjoyment for the friends. Many years ago Marilyn was asked to speak at a ladies luncheon in Torrance, California, and Luci indicated that she would like to drop in on her lunch hour to listen to her presentation. However, Marilyn *did not* want Luci to drop in and tried desperately to convince her that it was a minor speaking engagement and no big deal at all. Luci, though, was adamant: If she was in the area on her lunch break, she would simply drop in, listen, and then leave.

Finally, Marilyn schemed a plan that was sure to keep Luci far away from her luncheon. She told the determined Luci that she could come hear her speak if she wore a navy suit, carried her briefcase, chewed gum, stayed for thirty minutes, and wore her Mobil hard hat the entire time.

"Why on earth would I do that?" Luci asked incredulously.

(Earlier with friends they had been discussing a restaurant called The Hobbit, an incredibly expensive dining experience that required reservations seven months to a year in advance.) "Because if you do, I'll take you to The Hobbit as my guest," Marilyn coyly answered, confident her scheme had sufficiently scared Luci off.

The next day Marilyn sat at the head table, patiently enduring a fashion show of hand-sewn garments. "I was about to go into a coma," she laughs, "when I looked off into the anteroom and caught a glimpse of Luci in a blue suit, carrying a briefcase, and wearing her Mobil hard hat!" A slight murmur buzzed throughout the room as, one by one, the ladies saw the woman in the hard hat pacing in the lobby area. An anxious, concerned assistant organizer sped to the side of the chairman for a quick sidebar. Why on earth was there a representative from Mobil in their lobby? Marilyn bit her lip as the chairman zoomed to the lobby to investigate. Marilyn bit her lip harder for what she knew would come next.

The last and final condition that enabled Luci entrance to the luncheon was that she was not allowed to speak to anyone. If someone approached her, she would have to respond to them with a feigned speech impediment. Marilyn nearly burst watching the chairman trying to extricate information from the poker-faced Mobil employee. Confused, the chairman returned to her seat as her trusted assistant nervously asked what the woman said. "I don't know," a befuddled chairman responded. "The poor woman has some sort of speech defect." It was more than Marilyn could take as she sat twisting in her seat, suppressing her laughter and agonizing over the fact that Luci had beaten her.

Not to be outdone, Marilyn made her way to the podium to speak. With great concern she said, "I noticed there's a woman wearing a Mobil hard hat in the audience, and I wonder if there's a problem she needs to share?" Marilyn was sure Luci *would not* want to speak in front of the ladies. Without hesitation Luci marched to the front, earnestly digging for a scrap piece of paper in her suit pocket. With fully affected speech impediment, she confidently said, "Mobil Oil is digging a trench around the building to lay some pipes. The following cars will be smashed…" As women fumbled to find their keys and scraps of paper on which they may have written their license plate numbers, Luci rattled off bogus numbers "with full aplomb," Marilyn exclaims.

Unable to take the ruse any longer, Marilyn began laughing at Luci. The ladies, still in full swing of searching for their keys and license numbers stopped all activity and looked on in disbelieving horror as Marilyn laughed at a clearly handicapped woman! Beaten, Marilyn joyfully explained to her audience who Luci was and the conditions surrounding the bet. "They roared in applause for Luci but hated me!" Marilyn remembers. "And to make matters worse, nine months later I had to take Luci to The Hobbit."

Luci and Marilyn have long recognized the great possibility and potential of having fun together. As in most friendships, antics are rarely planned but happen spontaneously and usually occur in the most unlikely places. On a weekend when Marilyn's husband was to be out of town, she called Luci to see if she'd like to visit a church that was located near them. She had been curious to attend services there but didn't want to do it on a weekend she and her husband went to their own church together. They walked into the church lobby and were greeted by a very cordial usher who helped them to their seats.

The usher handed them each a visitor's card and informed them he would be by shortly to pick them up. Realizing they were simply visiting and

IT'S SO IMPORTANT TO LET YOUR FRIEND BE WHO SHE IS.

LUCI SWINDOLL

29

had no intention of leaving their own churches but not wanting the church visitation committee to spend time or effort tracking them down, Marilyn leaned over and whispered to Luci, "I'm not going to use my real name," and proceeded to write down the name of her deceased mother, Elizabeth Ricker, and her address in Washington. Luci wrote down the first name that popped into her head along with Marilyn's street address.

The usher came to collect the cards and Luci passed hers to Marilyn. Before handing both cards to the usher, Marilyn glanced briefly at Luci's card and chuckled at the name she had written: Bernadette Apes. The ladies sat back for a very enjoyable church service and flinched only slightly when the pastor said, "We've come to the time of our service that is my favorite…we're going to introduce our visitors." Marilyn immediately snickered but tried to remain poised. Luci whispered, "Marilyn, don't blow this. Just act like you're Elizabeth Ricker."

The kindhearted, friendly pastor began introducing the church guests one at a time. When he came to Elizabeth Ricker, Marilyn timidly raised her hand. Seeing she was from Vancouver, Washington, the pastor made lovely small talk about the majestic beauty of the area. Marilyn smiled politely and then breathed a sigh of relief when her turn was over. "He then came to my card," Luci offers, "and he paused."

"Miss Bernadette…Apes?" he said, trying to digest the name. Luci said nothing. "Bernadette Apes? Are you here, Miss Apes?" The congregation looked around uncomfortably. Luci finally raised her hand meekly.

"Miss Apes!" the pastor said victoriously. "We're so glad you're with us

today. We so always enjoy…" but before he could finish his verbal meandering,
Luci blurted out, "I'm a lonely woman!" Recovering from this shocking revela-
tion, the pastor slowly and lovingly said, "Well you've come to the right
place, Miss Apes." Luci made a few more inane comments, and then it was
over. Bernadette Apes was in the clear. Marilyn and Luci made a speedy exit
to the parking lot and fell over the car in hysterics.

The following Tuesday a man from the visitation
committee knocked on Marilyn's door. Her husband
Ken answered and was quick to let the man know that a
"Miss Bernadette Apes" did not live at that address. The
man showed the visitor's card with the name and
address to confirm he was at the right place. Ken said it
was the right address but he did not know a Miss Apes.
Closing the door, Ken made his way to a back bedroom

LUCI SWINDOLL & MARILYN MEBERG

where Marilyn was talking with their daughter. "Would you like to discuss
Bernadette Apes?" he casually asked his wife. "Not really," Marilyn answered.

After hearing the varied and absurd details of his wife's Sunday
escapades, he strongly suggested she and Luci apologize to the pastor.
"Marilyn called me and said, 'Ken thinks you should apologize,'" Luci remembers. "I said, 'I'm not apologizing. All I did was lie!'" she laughs. Buckling
beneath the guilt, Marilyn called the pastor and explained the story to him,
and to her great relief he laughed and laughed. "I think he was just so thankful there really *wasn't* a Bernadette Apes out there," Luci chuckles.

These friends have seen firsthand that laughter has a way of peeling

31

away layers of pretense and apprehension, thus opening a door to the soul and allowing a peek into someone's spirit. "I thrive on soul connection," Marilyn offers. "I am bored out of my mind with conversations that are just about the dailiness of life. I always want to know the whys of something rather than just the facts of something, and Luci is of the same mind. She makes me laugh, but she also makes me think."

"I search for the things in life that bring humor and joy—a light in the darkness," states Luci, "and I gravitate toward that sort of person as well. One of the reasons I love to be with Marilyn is because of her incredible joy. She's just a delight to be with."

In friendship you *should* delight in being with one another, and Luci and Marilyn clearly do. For these two, a friendship based on anything less would be no laughing matter.

For the past five years, Luci and Marilyn have been creating more hilarious memories for themselves while traveling with the Women of Faith conferences. They live only blocks away from each other in California, where they enjoy bicycling, talking, and yes, laughing with each other.

It is one of the blessings

of old friends that you can

afford to be stupid with them.

RALPH WALDO EMERSON

ARTHUR ASHE & STAN SMITH

Note: This story was written by Bob Briner.

*R*arely in the annals of sports has there been one single head-to-head rivalry that carried the entire sport to new heights as did the scintillating competition between Arthur Ashe and Stan Smith in the 1960s and '70s. It was so even, so compelling, and was played with such intensity and grace that it created and fueled the biggest boom the sport has even known. It even had New York taxi drivers talking about tennis—something they never did before.

Beneath what the public saw on tennis courts around the world was an even more compelling, enduring, and endearing phenomenon—one of the world's most beautiful friendships. Ultimately, it impacted both men to the extent that they walked through some of life's deepest valleys together.

Without tennis, or another of God's providences, it is very unlikely that Arthur and Stan would have even met. Arthur was from a gritty neighborhood on the outskirts of downtown Richmond, Virginia, in the then still segregated South, and Stan was the ultimate California golden boy. They lived a continent apart and light-years away in lifestyles. Tennis brought them together, and all kinds of sparks flew.

Because of the way tennis works, they played against each other almost constantly—that is, in the events that were desegregated, allowing Arthur to play. They were almost equal in ability—Arthur perhaps a littler quicker, Stan perhaps a little more powerful. It was impossible to tell who would win a match between them on a given day. It was a great rivalry. And they were great friends.

In those days, Arthur had a very low impression of Christianity. He felt that many of the people who called themselves Christians were the same ones who kept him from playing in many of the events important to his tennis career. In a memorable quote in *World Tennis Magazine*, Arthur said, "Jews, much more than Christians, have been kind and helpful as I have struggled with segregation in tennis." This was difficult to refute.

> WE ARE ALL TRAVELERS IN THE WILDERNESS OF THIS WORLD, AND THE BEST THAT WE FIND IN OUR TRAVELS IS AN HONEST FRIEND.
>
> ROBERT LOUIS STEVENSON

Stan Smith had become a solid believer in the Lord Jesus during his collegiate career at the University of Southern California. As they traveled the world, they spent virtually every day together—both in private and in the glare of spotlights and television—allowing Arthur an up-close-and-personal look at Stan's faith. What he found was consistency. If Stan won, he was gracious; and if he lost, he was just as gracious. If it was the middle Sunday of Wimbledon and all the other players were resting for the grueling second week, Stan was speaking in some London church. When Stan married, he married a beautiful young lady deeply committed to Christ. Stan was (and is) consistent.

How this consistency impacted Arthur was shown on a very dramatic evening in Dallas. Arthur and Stan had reached the finals of the biggest tournament of the year. This event, played before a packed house and before a vast worldwide television audience, had millions of dollars and the title "World Champion" riding on the outcome. As it happened, the whole match, the whole tournament, the entire tennis year was to be determined by one shot, a very dinky one at that. Arthur had caught Stan deep in his own back court and sought to win the match with a little drop shot barely over the net. It was a beautifully executed shot. It seemed to hit once and sort of die, but Stan, running, lunging, desperately reaching, got to the ball and flicked it over the net past Arthur. Now, the question was whether the ball was still "up," still good, when Stan hit it. No one really knew but Stan. Bedlam reigned in the arena. The chair umpire asked Stan if the shot was good, still playable, when he hit it. Stan said yes it was, and with that answer, Stan won the game, the set, the match, and the championship. In the post-match television interview, the announcer asked Arthur why he didn't protest and demand that the point be played over. His answer was memorable and telling: "If Stan said it was up, it was up." Wow! If Stan said it was up, it was up. With everything on the line, Stan's word could be trusted. Consistency.

All the above will provide context for the most important part of the Ashe-Smith relationship. One day in 1998 Arthur called and asked me to meet him at his beautiful and historic farmhouse in upstate New York. This was not unusual. He and I had worked there often on television projects. We had won Emmys for our joint efforts on the special "A Hard Road to Glory." But what he had to say to me that day was highly unusual. He told me he had contracted AIDS through a blood transfusion related to his ongoing heart problems. He said he wanted to keep this a secret so he could accomplish some things before the AIDS activists swooped down on him. He told me that Stan would also know, and he hoped that Stan and I would give him a crash course in the Scriptures, pray for him, and share our faith with him. From that point, Arthur and I were in contact most every day. I would fax him Scripture in the morning, and we would discuss it by phone in the afternoon. His calls would always begin this way: "Rab? Arthur. What's happening?" (My initials are RAB, and many people call me Rab.)

Stan and Margie Smith rearranged their schedule so they could be with Arthur and Jeanne on many weekends. Arthur's faith and understanding grew tremendously. His confidence in the future, in an eternal future, manifested itself in many ways. Larry King, on his television show, asked Arthur if he was a religious person and if he believed in life after death. "Yes," Arthur said on both counts. Before that, Arthur had assured me of his trust in Christ.

ARTHUR ASHE & BOB BRINER

A tremendous sadness comes over me when I realize I will never again pick up the phone and hear, "Rab? Arthur." But the sadness is quickly replaced by joy with the understanding that Arthur will never again need to ask, "What's happening?" Now he knows what's happening. He knows we love him. And he knows that his friend Stan Smith loves him as a brother.

Shortly after he wrote this story, Bob Briner lost his long battle with cancer. He was an Emmy award—winning television producer, the author of such books as Roaring Lambs, *and a tremendous friend to those of us who were fortunate enough to cross his path.*

DR. JOHNNY HUNT
ODUS SCRUGGS

During his freshman year of college, twenty-three-year-old Johnny Hunt had eagerly taken on the pastorate of a small local church in the rolling hills of North Carolina to support his family and pay his mounting college bills. It was in this beautiful rustic setting that he met Odus.

Odus Scruggs was a quiet, unpretentious seventy-year-old man and a dependable, faithful, behind-the-scenes person at the church when Johnny met him. "He would never be one to lead a class or an event," Johnny says in a smooth, southern voice, "but you could count on him being there in the background, doing his part in his own quiet way."

Retired from the power company, Odus and his wife, Viola, whom every-one lovingly referred to as "Punk," lived comfortably in a modest home. Their only children, twin boys, had died a few weeks after birth from kidney problems. "You had to pull conversation out of Odus," Johnny recalls, "but he would become another person around children. His whole face would light up. He absolutely loved and adored children!" Odus instantly befriended the new preacher and his young family. The congregation had a lot of older members, so when Odus saw Johnny and his family, he was as Johnny says, "overjoyed to see our children."

Johnny's father left when he was seven years old, leaving his mother to raise six children alone. Years of alcohol addiction began when Johnny was eleven, and high school was left behind for work in a pool hall when he was sixteen. "I never had a father figure," Johnny explains. "Odus met a great need in my life. He filled a very important role at that time." And at the same time, Johnny and his family were meeting a great need in the older couple's life. "We were the family they never got to have."

Johnny's meager salary at the church was barely enough to pay the electric bill let alone put food on the table, and Johnny and his young family were financially strapped. "We were so broke we couldn't pay attention," he laughs. Always sharply dressed, Odus called Johnny one day and said he wanted his help in picking out a new suit. "This wasn't unusual," Johnny relates. "Odus was always calling me to ride into town for something." Johnny patiently waited as Odus tried on suit after suit. After several had been properly color coordinated with shirt and tie, Odus asked for Johnny's honest opinion of which was the nicest. "Well, I like that one the best," Johnny said matter-of-factly, pointing to a well-made suit hanging on the rack. "I think that's the best one of the bunch." Turning to the salesman Odus said, "Get that suit in this man's size." Johnny adamantly refused such a generous gift but was quieted with words he has never forgotten: "Right now is the only time I have to show that I care," the old man said humbly.

> A FRIEND IS SOMEONE THAT IF THERE'S A CRISIS I KNOW I CAN CALL HIM AND I KNOW HE'D WANT ME TO CALL HIM.
>
> DR. JOHNNY HUNT

39

Odus would often call Johnny and invite his entire family out to eat. "And in those years nobody ever really went out to eat," Johnny exclaims. "That was high living!" On one of those many occasions as Johnny was turning down yet another invitation, Odus said something that Johnny still uses in his messages today. He simply said, "I want you to know I've never missed anything that I've given away." It was a powerful, life-changing lesson in servanthood for the young man. "To this day, the church I pastor is very generous and giving," Johnny offers. "Your first church allows you to cut your spiritual eyeteeth. Those early days of influence from men like Odus greatly shaped my life for future ministry."

Throughout the ensuing years of college, Odus continually reached for his wallet to help Johnny pay his bills. "He helped with groceries and gas and clothes for us and the kids," he says amazed. It was through Odus's constant, generous giving that Johnny learned how to receive as graciously as his friend gave. "It's hard to be on the receiving end," says Johnny. "But it's something Odus made me learn. But in all his giving, I never felt I owed Odus anything. He expected nothing in return from me. He never made any demands for anything. There was never any pretense with Odus. Never any ulterior motive. He simply chose to be a friend. And he was my *best* friend even though he was forty-seven years older than I was."

When Johnny finished college, in typical Odus fashion, he paid off the remainder of Johnny's college loan. A seven-hour drive separated the two men as Johnny headed off to seminary. "I suppose it was about a year later when Viola called and said Odus was in the cardiac-care unit," Johnny recalls. She told Johnny there didn't seem to be much hope and arranged for him to conduct the funeral. Knowing time away from seminary would be difficult, she didn't want him to come right away as no one was sure how long Odus would hold on in his present condition. Determined to see his friend again, Johnny jumped in his car and for seven hours prayed he'd have one more chance to see Odus and thank him for his friendship.

"The medical staff told me I could go in and see him but that he hadn't responded in days," remembers Johnny. The sight of his once-active friend dressed in a flimsy hospital gown and hooked to machines brought tears to Johnny's eyes as he stepped close to the bedside. "I bent down to his ear and said his name over and over," he recalls. The old man's eyes fluttered open, and recognizing his friend, he weakly said, "Johnny!" And though he was but a few short breaths from eternity, his enormous heart still overflowed with love as his fragile hand once again reached for his wallet. "That's what kind of man he was," Johnny says quietly. "His life taught me that people die as they live. Odus was a friend to the very end."

ODUS & VIOLA SCRUGGS

Smiling through his tears, Johnny thanked his sweet, godly friend for his friendship and influence in his life. "I said, 'Thank you for caring and believing in me,'" Johnny says evenly. "Everyone needs someone to believe in them, to encourage them. And Odus did. He was a once-in-a-lifetime friend."

Today Dr. Johnny Hunt pastors the eleven-thousand-member First Baptist Church of Woodstock, Georgia. On each side of his phone are pictures of the most influential people in his life: his mother and Odus Scruggs.

Everyone has a gift

for something, even if it is

the gift of being a good friend.

MARION ANDERSON

the gift of being a good friend

SOMEONE

WE CAN COUNT ON

NOTHING LIKE
A FRIEND

friendship

Someone we can count on

through the thick and thin

When the storms of life are blowing

there's just nothing like a friend

CHONDA PIERCE & ALISON EVANS

When a hurricane threatened to destroy homes in South Carolina, Alison Evans quickly told her husband that Chonda had said they could stay with her in Nashville till all danger had passed. Thinking a moment, Ken dryly replied, "You and Chonda in the same house…level-five hurricane…I'll take my chances with the hurricane."

The "Chonda" in question is comedian and author Chonda Pierce, and talking with her and best friend Alison is very much like having your very own hurricane whirling and spinning around you. "My husband is a nervous wreck when Chonda and I get together," Alison laughs. "He's socially very quiet, and the two of us together just throw him into a tailspin."

"We both love to talk," Chonda claims, putting great emphasis on the word *loooove*. "And we both have real strong personalities," adds Alison. "But, somehow, when we're together we just take turns, and it works!" Every friendship has a ritual or routine, something that only you and that particular friend like to do together or share a passion for. "We love oatmeal raisin cookies," says Alison. "We've been eating oatmeal raisin cookies and drinking Diet Pepsi as long as I can remember!" However, a love of conversation and a passion for oatmeal raisin cookies is where the similarities end.

Alison likes to get her hair colored professionally. "I, on the other hand, have been known to run to the store every now and then to buy a bottle to touch mine up a bit," laughs Chonda. Macy's department store is a little slice of heaven for Alison, while Chonda prefers Wal-Mart. She'll tell Alison, "You know, you could have gotten that same thing at Wal-Mart but without the same price tag!" Alison fondly remembers a time when she was helping Chonda decorate her house and they had to make a quick trip to Wal-Mart for something small. Chonda teased her and said, "You had to come all the way to Tennessee to shop at Wal-Mart so nobody you know would see you!"

Wal-Mart isn't the only thing these two don't have in common. "She's like a whirlwind," Alison states, "a flurry of activity. I can sit and do needlework for hours, and there's no way on this earth she could ever sit still long enough." Alison likes tailored clothing, while Chonda favors wild colors and prints. "You know, it's taken me years, but I think she dresses really nice now," Alison laughs. "I could never wear anything like that," she marvels, "but somehow it works for her!"

Alison is analytical, while Chonda is more fly-by-the-seat-of-her-pants. Alison loves the *Andy Griffith Show* and can recite episodes by heart. "She knows more quotes from the *Andy Griffith Show* than she does the Bible," Chonda says laughing. "I know more from the Bible, and she's always telling me to lighten up my spiritual load!" Talking about their differences makes both women laugh. Laughter is something they definitely have in common.

This boisterous friendship began when they were girls of eleven at youth camp. "We've been friends for a long time, but it's only since we've been married that we've been, as my husband says, 'joined at the hip,'" Chonda says chuckling. "I like friendship that has a past to it, and with Alison there's a definite connection."

These two friends have shared a lot of "past" together. When she was still a young girl, Chonda's twenty-year-old sister, Charlotta, was killed in a car accident. Just a little more than twenty months later, her fifteen-year-old sister, Cheralyn, died from a short bout of leukemia. "I was timid and shy about committing to a friendship after the death of my sisters, but Alison was very patient," offers Chonda. "I am blessed to have a lot of friends, but Alison is the one who really knows me."

When Alison's son was still an infant, Alison was offered a job opportunity in South Carolina, closer to family. While their Nashville home was put on the market, Alison took her son to South Carolina as her husband stayed behind to sell the house. "Now keep in mind," Chonda says, "we did everything together. Our husbands got along, so we'd do things as a foursome. Sometimes I would baby-sit their son; we were very, very close." But as time went by, Chonda and her husband noticed that the "For Sale" sign was no longer up at Alison's house. "We dropped in on her husband to see how things were going, and later we called Alison to get an update. The story he was telling her was that 'Houses are moving real slow in Nashville right now.'" Over time, Chonda made the very painful discovery that Alison's husband was being unfaithful. "Blatantly unfaithful," Chonda says pointedly. "It seems his unfaithfulness was known to everyone but us."

After much thought and many discussions with her husband, Chonda knew she had to call Alison. "That was so hard," she says slowly. "I had to call her and break the news to her about her husband's infidelities. I knew I was risking the friendship to tell her the truth."

Alison vividly remembers the day she got the phone call. "Sometimes you want to shoot the messenger and not believe the story," she says. "But because we'd already been through so much together, I knew it had taken a lot of courage for Chonda to tell me the truth, which I think is a real benchmark for friendship. That's a much better friend than one who would try to shield you from the truth. Chonda knew the truth would hurt me but that I'd be hurt more if I didn't know."

"You can have friends who are yes people," says Chonda, "but that isn't healthy. Alison doesn't give me pep talks. She talks honestly with me, and I talk honestly with her. I made that phone call knowing there would be embarrassment issues to deal with and the whole 'Why didn't you tell me sooner?' aspect; but somehow, our friendship survived it. We stand amazed that our friendship endured." The following years were

SHE KEEPS MY LIFE REAL. THAT'S WHAT FRIENDS DO— THEY KEEP YOUR FEET ON THE GROUND.

CHONDA PIERCE

ones of struggle and pain as Alison was thrust into the oftentimes harsh world of a working single mother. Chonda grieved with her friend as her marriage ended. "It was devastating and gut-wrenching to watch her go through it," Chonda says soberly. "But I was also able to rejoice with her when she began seeing a wonderful man who years later would become her husband and the father of her little boy."

They both agree that one of the reasons their friendship has lasted so long is that they base it on unconditional love. "Either one of us could do the dumbest thing in the world, but the other one would still be there," says Alison. "Of course that doesn't mean we wouldn't tell each other that was the dumbest thing in the world!" And neither is intimidated to tell the other the truth. "If I show her something new I'm considering for my act, she'll be the first to laugh the hardest or tell me it's not funny," states Chonda. Chonda recalls a humorous moment of truth when she and her husband were going through a tough period. "It was one of those rough spots that all marriages go through, and Alison came to Nashville to see me. But," she says laughing, "she says she didn't come to save the marriage but to keep me from killing my husband...to keep me out of prison!"

Since they were young girls of eleven, Chonda and Alison have tried to share nearly everything together. They've been poor together: "One time we dug through drawers, pants pockets, and the car seats looking for money to buy a box of oatmeal raisin cookies and some fake champagne for a celebration," Chonda says laughing. They've been pregnant together: "We were big and pregnant and got lost in the Vanderbilt library. We waddled around that place for two hours looking for each other," states Alison. "I finally just sat on the floor in tears! It was horrible." Chonda claims, "She went into labor while we were watching *The Ghost of Mr. Chicken* and refused to go to the hospital until it was over!" They've vacationed together: "We went to the beach, and for a week we memorized all the answers to a Trivial Pursuit–type game just so we could beat our husbands," Alison laughs. And they've spent countless hours together: "We've invested a lot of time in each other," Chonda offers. "We've worked *hard* at this friendship."

CHONDA PIERCE &
ALISON EVANS

"We're not trying to get something out of the relationship," she continues. "We're just blessed because we have it."

Alison is a licensed professional counselor and lives in South Carolina with her husband and teenage son, Justin. In April 2000, Chonda received the prestigious Grady Nutt Humor Award presented by the Gospel Music Association for excellence in comedic achievement. Alison was there as Chonda received her honor.

In friendship we find

nothing false or insincere:

everything is straightforward

and springs from the heart.

CICERO

everything

is straightforward

springs from the heart

heart

POINT OF GRACE

SHELLEY BREEN AND DENISE JONES

Shelley Breen met fellow Point of Grace member Denise Jones during their freshman year in college. "My first memory of her is sitting next to her in church and how loud she sang," Shelley says lightheartedly. "It's funny how I turned out to be the loudmouth!"

Majoring in music, both girls auditioned for a popular all-girl, touring, singing group. Competition was stiff, as only thirteen or fourteen girls would make the final cut. The girls would be required to sing and dance onstage, so a short dance routine would be taught at the audition. Born with two left feet, Shelley dreaded the audition. When she arrived that day, she discovered that she had *missed* the dance-routine instructions. "It was hopeless!" she laughingly remembers. Picking up what she could from watching the other girls, Shelley confined herself to a corner to hammer out the steps on her own. Pitying her pathetic floundering and flailing, sweet-natured Denise graciously offered to help Shelley learn the routine. "She was so good, she could have taught the class!" Shelley exclaims. After Denise's one-on-one dancing lesson, Shelley auditioned and miraculously made the group. "Most girls wouldn't want to help the competition, but Denise must have seen that I really wasn't any competition and took pity on me!" Shelley quit the group after that first year. "It was such a struggle to do that dancing!" she blurts. "But Denise sang and danced her way through all four years."

Long bus rides and lengthy tours have enabled Shelley to see her friend as the genuinely sweet person she came to know her as in college. "After the rest of us have taken off our makeup and are on the bus and ready to go, she's the one who is still inside the lobby talking with people!"

Many years of shared experiences in college and on the road have strengthened their long relationship. "She knows me for me," states Shelley. "My relationship with her really keeps me grounded. We were friends before there even was a Point of Grace, and I know she'll always be there for me—no matter what."

Shelley lives in Nashville with her husband and one of her best friends, their cocker spaniel, Snickers.

DENISE JONES AND LAURA WELCH

Some friends leave an indelible mark on our lives through their quiet dignity, strength, and optimism. Laura Welch has left such a mark on Denise Jones. "She's endured so much pain, yet you'd never know anything was

SHE HELPS ME REMEMBER WHERE I CAME FROM, WHERE MY ROOTS ARE, AND WHO I AM AS A PERSON.

DENISE JONES

wrong because she's always so emotionally strong and thankful," Denise says, amazed.

The girls met in a third-grade Sunday school class in Norman, Oklahoma. Short, diminutive Denise was immediately drawn to the tall, dark haired, freckle-faced girl's exuberance, imagination, and love of life. "We'd play together at her house, and there was always something fun to do because she just drew me into her wonderful, creative world."

When Denise's sister and Laura's brother began dating in high school, their parents sent the then fifth graders along as chaperones. "They called us 'videotape' because we'd tell everything they did," Denise laughs.

However, their carefree days of childhood would often be interrupted by Laura's diabetes. "There would be long stretches of time when she wasn't around because she was so sick," recalls Denise. But Denise soon realized that her friend couldn't be kept down for long. "Laura is one of those people who keeps going against all odds," she marvels. And the odds have often been stacked against her friend. She's gone through both kidney and pancreatic transplant surgeries, has lost nearly all her eyesight, and is now mostly con- fined to a wheelchair. "But her attitude is always one of thankfulness," states Denise. "She's such a positive influence on me because she's so thankful to God for allowing her to use her diabetes to help others! She loves to say to them, 'Yes, you can live with this disease and have a positive outlook,' because she's actually been there and done it!" Denise exclaims.

Though distance and schedules keep the friends from visiting regularly in person, they remain close in heart. "She's taught me how to cherish people in my life," says Denise, "and she's taught me that every moment is a gift from God. She doesn't take time for granted, and I hope I can be like that—really cherishing each and every moment."

Moments that, oftentimes, only a friend can teach.

Denise lives in Nashville with her husband, Stu, and their sons, Spence and Price. Laura's dream is to work in a children's hospital, counseling children with diabetes.

> A TRUE FRIEND ALLOWS YOU TO BE NOTHING BUT YOURSELF—LETTING IT ALL HANG OUT—AND CONTINUES TO LOVE YOU, FAULTS AND ALL.
>
> TERRY JONES

TERRY JONES AND KRISTI JENKINS

When Terry Jones and her boyfriend broke up in college, it was her roommate who helped her through a very emotional roller-coaster ride. "She's always been a godly woman," Terry says of her friend Kristi Jenkins. "Her walk with Christ has always encouraged me, and she's always held me accountable." Honest, straightforward Kristi helped keep Terry focused on God during the painful breakup.

On November 27, 1999, Point of Grace was on tour when Terry retrieved a message off of her home answering machine from an old college suite mate. What had been a healthy pregnancy for the petite 5'1" Kristi had taken a sudden and traumatic turn as she gave birth to her baby son. "Complications arose almost immediately, and they had to perform an emergency C-section," Terry recalls. "They took the baby, who was

KRISTI JENKINS & TERRY JONES

healthy, but Kristi kept bleeding internally and her uterus wouldn't contract." As Kristi lay heavily sedated, her husband had to make on-the-spot decisions. In order to stop the bleeding, a hysterectomy was performed, and Kristi continued to receive several blood transfusions. However, by Saturday night doctors realized she was going into full-blown DIC, a high-fatality bleeding disorder in which clotting factors are used somewhere else in the body rather than where they're needed. "When I got the message on the road," Terry recalls, "I went to the other Point of Grace girls and said, 'We have to pray.' When things like that happen, you realize that time is so short and how precious life is."

After five days in ICU, Kristi finally got to hold her baby in her arms. Nine days and 150 units of blood later, she was transferred to the progressive care unit, where she continued to bleed. A CT scan revealed a lacerated spleen that was causing some of the bleeding. Kristi was finally released from the hospital three weeks later. "I think it's because of the prayers of family and friends that Kristi walked out of the hospital alive," Terry says reverently. "I really believe that God heard the prayers of those faithful prayer warriors," Kristi offers. "I always knew that Terry was praying for me and that has had a great impact on our friendship."

"When you face the potential death of someone you love, it makes you so much more thankful for that person," Terry states. "I'm a better Christian because of Kristi—I'm better as a result of her being there."

Terry actually went on to marry the boyfriend who broke her heart in college, and today they're the proud parents of Cole and Luke. Kristi only recently returned to work as a lab technician as her body continues to heal from the trauma that happened in 1999. She and her husband cherish each day they have together with their son—also named Cole.

HEATHER PAYNE AND JASA BABB

George Eliot said that friendships begin with liking or gratitude. Sometimes we meet someone who is totally different from us, yet we somehow manage to find a spark, a connection in each other that is nothing more than genuine likability.

Heather Payne was a busy music major when Jasa Babb transferred to Ouachita Baptist College her sophomore year. "We ended up as suite mates," Heather recalls, "but other than that, I never really got to know her." Jasa's grandmother had been praying that she would find a sweet, godly friend who would be a kindred spirit, but that close, deep relationship seemed constantly out of reach.

Circumstances changed during their junior year when Heather came down with mono and was unable to attend classes. "Jasa happened to be around one day, and we ended up going to lunch together," reflects Heather. For well over a year Heather had assumed that she and Jasa had nothing in common: "She grew up on a dairy farm; I grew up in the city. She hates to shop, and I love it. I'm tall with brown hair, and she's a petite blonde. We're just very, very opposite." But after a four-hour lunch, the

girls discovered that they had much in common as they discussed families, God, and things they'd never voiced to any other friend. "Those four hours we spent talking that day were a milestone in our friendship," Heather states. "We realized that although we didn't share many external interests, we did share our relationship with the Lord and we were like-minded in our love for Him—and that created an everlasting friendship."

HEATHER PAYNE & JASA BABB

Nearly ten years later, Heather found herself in a quandary: She was engaged and would be married in just one month. "My sister couldn't make the trip to the wedding. She lived in Colorado and was nine months pregnant," says Heather. "I was maid of honor in Jasa's wedding and knew she was the only person I'd choose to take the place of my sister as my matron of honor."

"You have different degrees of friends," she continues. "I think I love Jasa the way Jonathan loved David, and I know she loves me the same way. We would sacrifice for each other." Regardless of differences, that's the best degree of friend there is.

Heather and her husband, Brian, are currently making their home in Alabama as Brian finishes seminary. Jasa and her husband, Buddy, live with their two children in Arkansas.

We all need sheltering trees

Friends in our lives

who'll get down on their knees

And lift us up before

the King of Kings

We all need sheltering trees

WE ALL NEED

FRIENDS WHO

LIFT US UP

friendship

DWIGHT WATSON & RON FROST

*L*oneliness can devastate even the strongest life. Over an extended period, it can deaden the soul and paralyze the human spirit. In 1986, NewSong Road Pastor Dwight Watson was facing the crippling effects of loneliness. The thirteen-year-old's life was reeling out of control, and he felt—in a word—friendless. "I didn't just *feel* like I didn't have friends," Dwight recalls. "I really *didn't* have any friends."

The straggly haired, unkempt youth had had various disciplinary problems, served in-school suspension, and been suspended from the bus more times than he could remember. He had been justifiably dropped from accelerated classes, and his sore, calloused attitude and frequent lying continually got him into trouble. He lied even if he knew he couldn't gain anything by it. He lied to get out of trouble, and he lied to get *into* trouble—any attention was better than no attention at all. At every turn, Dwight was driving a wedge between himself and others and feeling more and more alone.

Raised one of three children by a single mother, the troubled boy longed for a strong male role model in his life. "I never actually knew who my father was," he states. "All the men in my life seemed to disappear as soon as I grew attached to them."

Living just beyond the fringe of social acceptance, Dwight never fit in with his peers. One boy did occasionally hang out with him when they weren't at school—but only on the condition that Dwight wouldn't tell anyone they were friends. "That was the deal," he remembers. "Of course I was so starved for attention that that didn't bother me."

At the end of his seventh-grade year, Dwight looked forward to entering middle school because kids he'd never met from other schools would now be combined into one. "I was determined to make friends," he says. But hopes for approval and a sense of belonging were soon abandoned as Dwight found himself gravitating to others like himself. At fourteen, the young boys he loosely called his friends were already into drugs, alcohol, and promiscuous activities. "It was a pretty rough crowd," Dwight recalls. Too frightened of their effects, Dwight avoided drugs; and life with several alcoholic men deterred his use of alcohol as well. Realizing that his avoidance of drugs and alcohol might ruin his chance of fitting in with even this group, Dwight found something that set him apart and won their approval.

"One day we were in a convenience store, and I grabbed a candy bar or something and shoved it in my pocket," Dwight says. His buddies thought his action was the smoothest, coolest move they'd seen. "I knew it was wrong the very moment I did it," Dwight says pointedly. "I can't say I was the victim of circumstances, because I knew exactly what I was doing—but I was so starved for attention that I was willing to do anything to get it. It was a way I could be cool." Dwight honed his thieving skills in convenience stores and gas stations and then moved on to breaking into businesses and homes. "It became my drug," he states matter-of-factly. "At first I did it to impress my friends, but after a while, it turned into a challenge; and I did it to see if I could get away with it."

Most criminals leave the site of their crime and never return. Dwight, however, broke into homes in his area several times. While riding his moped one day, Dwight was forced to stop when Ron Frost, a homeowner in his neighborhood, stepped out of the woods into his path. Ironically, the twenty-something Ron looked at him and said, "Dwight, I thought you were my friend." Scraping the bottom of his shoe over the moped's pedal, Dwight mumbled, "I don't have any friends." Ron answered wryly, "I really want to be your friend, but it's hard when you keep breaking into my house." He was caught. Dwight wasn't sure how Ron knew, but now he was trapped.

The homeowners in his area had gotten together and were determined to press charges against the young delinquent. "Ron somehow convinced them to let him handle it," Dwight says in astonished wonder. Ron looked at the hardened boy and said, "What do you think we should do about this?"

"I guess we better go call the police," Dwight replied.

Ron shook his head, "No, that's not what we're going to do."

Dwight suddenly became frightened. Was Ron planning to take matters into his own hands? Would he physically punish him and leave him here in this wooded area?

"I'll make a deal with you," Ron said calmly. "If you'll go to church with me for four weeks, I won't call the authorities."

"Even in my twisted way of thinking," Dwight says, "I knew that was a much better option than the alternative."

For the next three weeks, Ron and his wife, Kathy, picked Dwight up for church, took him to lunch, dropped him off, and then picked him up again for evening services. Young Dwight was amazed at how well he was treated by Ron and his wife. "They treated me better than my own family," he exclaims. At each service Dwight heard about God's love and grace and acceptance, but he couldn't bring himself to believe it. "I didn't feel that anyone loved me, much less God," he states.

> FRIENDSHIP IS A RELATIONSHIP IN WHICH THE GREATEST CONCERN IS THE BENEFIT OF THE OTHER PERSON—NOT YOURSELF AND WHAT YOU CAN GET OUT OF THE FRIENDSHIP.
>
> DWIGHT WATSON

Two weeks into "the deal," the annual youth summer camp was announced, and Ron asked if Dwight had plans to go. Knowing it would be financially impossible, Dwight shook his head no. A few days later, he received a call from the youth pastor of the church saying that his way to summer camp had been paid. "I've never known who paid my way, but I have a hunch," he says with a smile.

Over time it became clear that Ron wasn't concerned in getting anything back that Dwight had stolen from his home. "He wasn't interested in retribution," Dwight says, "which is the American way—you know, getting even. He wasn't concerned with any of that. His only concern was me."

Driving home from church the day before leaving for camp, Dwight looked at Ron and said, "I don't understand why you've done all this for me. Anyone else would have taken me to jail, yet you've treated me like a son. Why?"

BACK L-R: KATHY & RON FROST,
DWIGHT & KATIE WATSON
FRONT L-R: CORINNA & OLIVIA FROST

Tears swam in Ron's eyes as he simply said, "Because I love you." Uncertain of how to react, Dwight sat quietly and pondered Ron's response. He had never heard someone say those words to him. "Ron wasn't just saying it," he states reflectively. "He was living it." It was at that moment that God's love became real to Dwight, and His grace, mercy, and unconditional love were clearly understood. "He's the person who actually showed me God's love—the first person who made God's love real to me. He helped nurture me, spent time with me, and made me feel important because I was important to him. I saw God's love in him, and that was the first time I had ever seen that in my life!"

In early 2000, Dwight was asked to speak at Ron's ordination ceremony into ministry. "Ron always claims he's not a good public speaker," Dwight says he told the crowd, "but before he ever preached a sermon from a pulpit, he was preaching from his life through his actions. That's what impacted and changed my life, and that's what will impact *any* life."

Throughout the years, Ron and Dwight's relationship has transitioned out of a close mentorship into a rich friendship, but during those formative years were immeasurable lessons in compassion, patience, love, and the value and worth of each person. "The greatest thing I've learned from Ron's friendship," Dwight states plainly, "is the importance of people and to love them—like Christ loves them—no matter what they look like or whether they deserve it. I sure didn't deserve it, but I was important to Ron!" As important as a friend.

In late 2000, Ron, Kathy, and their two daughters moved to Spain to work as church planters. Dwight and his wife, Katie, are newlyweds and are following God's call on their lives, working in youth ministry and the arts.

CLOUDS
OF DOUBT

CAME
ROLLING IN

friendship

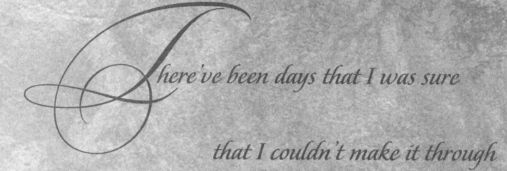

There've been days that I was sure

that I couldn't make it through

Clouds of doubt came rolling in

and I didn't know what I would do

STORMIE OMARTIAN & ROZ THOMPSON

We've all come to learn that life is no respecter of people. You can be peacefully sailing along when suddenly your tiny sail is assaulted by a raging storm. Before you're able to steady your little boat, gale-force winds whir it, spin it, and knock it about on what was once a calm sea. Harsh winds can come in the form of a lost job, financial difficulties, marital problems, sickness, etc. Trapped in the eye of the storm, your mind races to the list of people you can call on for help. It's then that you realize your list is chiefly comprised not of friends, but of glorified acquaintances. As you scan the list, your heart stops at only a name or two—the names of people you know will drop anything at anytime to help you through any problem. They're the ones you call, and with barely a whisper you say, "Will you pray?" and they do. And regardless of the problem, they're beside you, helping you, strengthening you, encouraging you, praying for you.

More than fifteen years ago, best-selling author and speaker Stormie Omartian and her husband, record producer Michael Omartian, attended a prayer group for people who worked in the secular entertainment industry at their church, Church on the Way in Van Nuys, California. Through the crowded room Stormie spotted Roz Thompson, a beautiful African-American woman. "She looked like a queen," Stormie recalls. "She's tall and has a gorgeous face. An absolutely royal face." Stormie, who was at the meeting because of her husband's profession, knew why the striking Roz was also part of the evening. "I'd heard her sing in church, and she had the most beautiful voice," Stormie says in deep admiration.

The two women struck up a conversation, and Stormie was astounded at the genuine humility the unbelievably talented Roz displayed. "She actually said, 'This is so intimidating. This is a group for talented people. I shouldn't be here.' And she meant it. She was genuinely humble," says Stormie. Yet Roz's vast résumé of work soundly rang of her talent. Years earlier she had been the opening act for Bill Cosby, the Smothers Brothers, Bob Newhart, and other top comedians in Las Vegas and Tahoe. She traveled with comedian Paul Lynde and had performed several times on *The Tonight Show* with Johnny Carson, on *The Merv Griffin Show*, and on *The Flip Wilson Show*. She'd worked on television specials with Burt Bacharach and Marvin Hamlish and performed in the L.A. touring show of *The Wiz* and other musicals.

"I was attracted to her diversity," remembers Stormie. "She grew up at a time of racial injustice, yet she was so kind. She had such a beautiful spirit." As the two women talked, they realized the similar history and abundance of interests they had in common. "We understood each other because we shared so many hurts from the past," Stormie states. "Even our husbands shared many experiences because they both worked in the music industry. It encouraged us both to know that we weren't alone in some of the things we were going through in our marriages. All those experiences instantly bonded us."

Stormie asked Roz if she'd like to be a part of her prayer group, and fifteen years later the friends are still praying together. "I'd had a prayer life before I met Stormie," Roz says, "but nothing like it is now. She's helped me understand the concept of bathing everything in my life in prayer."

"And," Stormie adds, "when someone is transparent and you see where their hurts are, you can't help but love them. Then when you pray for that person, your love grows even more. Even if you'd previously had a negative attitude about that person, it will change to love." Stormie and Roz soon learned that nothing in their lives would create a greater bond between them than praying together.

In 1993 the ladies saturated their lives with prayer as both their husbands were toying with the idea of moving from California. "I told her Michael was thinking of moving his studio to Nashville, and she said, 'Chester's talking about moving to Nashville too,' recalls Stormie. "We couldn't believe it." Within a few short months, both families were enjoying the beauty of middle Tennessee and suffering from the allergies that often plague the area. "I'd never even had allergy or sinus problems," says a stuffy-nosed, weak-voiced Roz, ailing again from a sinus infection. "I moved here and was immediately attacked full force."

Three short years later, Roz checked into a local hospital for what was supposed to be a minor laprascopic surgery to remove an ovary. "I was supposed to go home the next morning," she remembers. However, doctors discovered that instead of the simple laser procedure, they would actually have to cut into her—but she would still be released the next day. The surgery went well, and once Roz was awake in the recovery room, they wheeled her back to her own room. By her bedside was a bouquet of flowers and get-well wishes. "I don't know if the flowers triggered an allergic reaction or what," Roz says slowly, "but I spiraled down quickly."

Baffling the doctors, Roz's earlier postoperative strength was quickly deteriorating. Her condition worsened so rapidly that the medical staff whirred her past her worried husband to the critical care unit, where they discovered she had full-blown pneumonia. "It all happened too fast to process," recalls Roz. "I went down so quickly that I was never really aware of what was happening."

> THERE IS TRUE LOYALTY BETWEEN US. I CAN DEPEND ON HER, AND SHE CAN DEPEND ON ME. YOU CAN'T SAY THAT ABOUT EVERYONE IN LIFE, USUALLY ONLY ONE OR TWO FRIENDS.
>
> STORMIE OMARTIAN

What should have been an overnight visit ended up as a ten-day, round-the-clock watch in the hospital. Stormie was on the road speaking when she heard the news. "I talked to her on the phone," she says, "and she sounded so bad I barely recognized her voice. But I had no idea how bad she was until I saw her." Apparently, the optimistic Roz never had a full understanding of how serious her condition was until her seventeen-year-old son, Akil, was allowed to visit. "When I looked at his face, I thought, *Am I dying?* It was then that I realized I must be in really bad shape."

As soon as Stormie flew back into Nashville, she organized the ladies in their prayer group to visit their sick friend the very next morning. At 8:00

A.M., Stormie and two other prayer warriors marched into the critical-care unit to cover Roz in prayer. Hospital policy allowed only one visitor at a time to visit critical-care patients. "We told the nurse we were her prayer group, and she let all three of us in!" Stormie exclaims. The God Squad, as Roz would later call them, immediately went to work. "Her room was filled with flowers," Stormie says. "I thought, *With all her allergy problems, why are all these flowers in here?* and I immediately took them out of her room!" Roz was aware of her friends' presence but could barely respond to them. "She was so weak she couldn't even lift her hand," remembers Stormie.

The God Squad took their places on all sides of Roz's bed and bathed her with prayer for more than an hour. "We interceded for her and let the devil have it," Stormie laughs emphatically. "When you're led by the Spirit, it's beyond you, and you pray as the Spirit leads—and that's what we did." As the group prayed, Roz detected a beautiful fragrance in the room that was unlike anything she'd ever smelled. Later, she commented to the ladies that they were wearing beautiful perfume. They realized none of them was wearing any perfume at all. "It had to be the fragrance of the Lord filling my room," Roz says. At the end of their prayers, Roz felt something break in her body. "I felt a remarkable difference take place," she says amazed. "It was a lifting, a release." By the end of their prayer, she was breathing more freely, sitting up, and asking for something to eat. "It was absolutely incredible," Stormie says quietly. "It was just remarkable. The doctors and nurses were shocked."

Through the prayer of friends, Roz left the hospital just a few days later. "I'm sure it could be argued that the time spent in critical care had run its course, that the medicines and care given had worked; but it wasn't until they prayed over me that I felt a difference, a tremendous release." Stormie entered the critical-care unit confident that if it was God's will, He was able to relieve Roz from the clutches of sickness. "Sometimes we forget the authority we have in the Lord," Roz offers. "But Stormie has a consistent understanding of that power and of who we are in the Lord."

ROZ THOMPSON & STORMIE OMARTIAN

Over the years the friends have launched many powerful prayer maneuvers on each other's behalf and know in their hearts how to intercede for one another. "She knows how to pray for me," Stormie offers, "and I know how to pray for her. She's confident that prayer works, and I can always depend on her to pray. She has such a heart for her son and my children. She prays for my children as if they were her own, and I do the same for her." Each woman often knows how to pray for the other long before a need is evident. "Stormie has a way of seeing something and nipping it in the bud," reflects Roz. "She'll see something in my life, pray over it, and then lovingly confront me; and I can do the same for her. Even after all the accolades and successes, Stormie doesn't act as if she's got it all together. She believes in her heart that apart from the Lord she can do nothing. She knows that she can't do anything until she takes it to the Lord. That prayerful attitude has made a powerful difference in my life."

Two years ago Stormie saw the beauty and felt the power of her praying friend as she herself was taken to the hospital. For reasons unknown, she found herself doubled over in pain in the middle of the night. Alone for the weekend and unable to drive herself to the hospital, she called her grown son and her sister Suzy, who immediately called Roz to pray. Awakened from sleep, Roz instinctively said, "I'm going there," and in the dark of night drove twelve miles to the hospital. "She was waiting for us when we got there," a moved Stormie says. "I was so touched. That's what a *friend* does. That kind of friend is rare. A friend is someone you can call in the middle of the night to pray and she says, 'I'm going *there* to pray.' *That's* a close friend! People have very few friends like that in a whole lifetime. Those are the kind of friends you need. You don't need a million of them—just one or two."

Stormie has written ten books. Her two books on prayer, The Power of a Praying Wife *and* The Power of a Praying Parent, *have collectively sold more than 1.4 million copies. She lives in Nashville with her husband and has three grown children. Roz conducts a nationwide seminar called B.A.T.T.L.E. (Bringing Attention to the Lord's Excellence) that focuses on the differences between praise and worship. She and her husband, Chester—drummer for the group Genesis and for pop artist Phil Collins—also live in Nashville and have two grown children.*

A faithful friend is a strong defense;

And he that hath found him

hath found a treasure.

LOUISA MAY ALCOTT

I would've given in

and said I just can't go on

If it hadn't been for a friend

that helped me to be strong

I WOULD'VE GIVEN IN

IF IT HADN'T BEEN FOR A FRIEND

friendship

CAROLYN ARENDS & BERNIE SHEAHAN

*N*o matter how many self-help books you read, motivational tapes you listen to, or inspirational episodes of *Oprah* you watch, sometimes it's hard to look yourself in the mirror and say in total confidence, "I believe in you. You can do it!" Sometimes everything in your mind and soul is crying out, "Are you crazy? You can't do that!" But then, right when you've convinced yourself you'll never be anything more than someone who talks to herself in the mirror, a friend will say, "Have you ever thought of trying…? I think you'd be really good at it." And just as quickly as the doubts and anxieties swelled to a frenzied peak, they begin to subside with the simple belief of a friend.

Carolyn Arends never talked to herself in the mirror, but the doubts were still there, gently rooting themselves in the subterranean regions of her mind and heart. The busy contemporary Christian singer/songwriter/author met Bernie Sheahan at a time in her life when she thought she probably wouldn't make any more close friends. "My life already felt full: I had some close friendships, and I didn't think I'd develop any new ones. But God put Bernie in my path, and she's someone who believes with all her heart that I can do something. She has consistently encouraged me in different aspects of my life."

For several years before they met, they shared mutual friends who would tell each of them, "You really need to meet Carolyn. You'll love her," or "You've got to meet Bernie. You two would really hit it off." But regardless of how many mutual friends they had, their paths never crossed until a few years later. "I was working on my second record," Carolyn recalls, "and the record company was having Bernie write my bio. She came into the room where I was working, and we connected immediately because we're both right brained…or is it left brained? We were both the side of the brain that finds it easier to write stories than remember which side of the brain is which and where you left the car keys. We connected on a creative level and could laugh about locking the keys in the car *again!*"

When Carolyn was on an extended tour with Steven Curtis Chapman and Audio Adrenaline, she found herself surrounded by men with the exception of only one other crew woman whom she seldom saw. "There must have been fifty guys on that tour," she laughs. "And me!" Single, fun-loving Bernie would jump into her battered BMW, which she affectionately called the "Dude Magnet," and would drive to many of the concerts on the tour. "She'd pick me up, and we'd ride alongside the buses to the next concert, laughing

A GREAT FRIEND IS ASTONISHINGLY VERSATILE: A PLACE OF COMFORT AND AN AGENT OF CHANGE, A SOFT SHOULDER AND THE IRON THAT SHARPENS IRON. PLUS, A FRIEND WILL TELL YOU IF YOU HAVE SPINACH IN YOUR TEETH…BUT IN THE NICEST WAY POSSIBLE.

CAROLYN ARENDS

and talking the entire way there." Unfortunately, the Dude Magnet died early in the friendship, so Carolyn never really got to bond with it. "Most of the trip," she says laughing at the absurdity of the name, "took place in Dude Magnet II."

Riding together on those trips began what Carolyn calls "the growing-up phase" of their relationship. "In the first phase of the friendship, we clearly recognized our similarities. In the second phase we began to recognize our differences and really appreciate the uniqueness of the other person." At first, the gregarious, outgoing, passionate Bernie slightly overwhelmed the quiet, unassuming Carolyn. "She's over-the-top," Carolyn explains, "but in a good way. But it's still a way that's really out there compared to me." Bernie would teasingly call Carolyn "a shy Canadian Baptist." But whatever differences the women saw between them, everyone else saw only stunning similarities. "People started calling us the Wonder Twins," Carolyn recalls, "although we look nothing alike or act anything alike." But they do tend to think alike...

On a working trip to Nashville, Carolyn and Bernie were at Carolyn's management office when Carolyn realized she needed something from a nearby mall. "It was only the first or second time Bernie and I were together," she remembers, "so we were still in that 'discovering the similarities' phase." As they were leaving for the mall, a virtual downpour of rain descended from the sky. "It was coming down in buckets," laughs Carolyn. "Someone in the management office gave us two ball caps that said 'Stay Calm' on the front of them." Pulling their caps tight onto their heads, they headed out the door and jumped into the Dude Magnet for the drive to the mall. The drive there would afford them the extra time they needed to finish a conversation they had already begun. "We were talking about school," Carolyn reflects, "and about doing well in school." She laughs as she continues. "We were talking about the fact that we had each skipped a grade in school. It's embarrassing to admit this, but I guess that in a way we were talking about how smart we were!"

Running through sheets of rain, they trudged into the mall, shaking off excess water as they looked for The Bombay Company. "We were still talking about school when we both spotted a really cool pencil box. I picked it up and said, 'But once you sharpen the pencils, they'll be too big for the box,'" Carolyn groans as she remembers the moment. "Bernie looked at it and said, 'Yeah, they won't fit anymore.' Then it dawned on both of us what extreme idiots we were." Standing as soaked rats, their "Stay Calm" hats now somewhat soggy and askew, the two women who had effortlessly skipped grades in school laughed together at their inability to figure out the most basic principle of sharpening a pencil: Once sharpened it gets smaller *not* bigger. "We stood there and just laughed at ourselves," she remembers. "It is so healing to find someone who struggles with the same things you do. In our case—the everyday functions in life. Sharing a similar weakness with someone can bring great understanding and healing because you realize, 'I'm not the only one like this!'"

CAROLYN ARENDS & BERNIE SHEAHAN

As the friends drew closer together, they moved into what Carolyn calls the third phase of their friendship. "We are very intentional about our relationship," she says. "We live over two thousand miles apart and both live busy lives. It would be easy to simply talk only when I made a trip to Nashville, but we have consciously decided that we want to bear each other's burdens and constantly bring the other back to the feet of God. We've become accountable to each other. Bernie tends to think that I get overcommitted. She has said to me, 'Working this hard isn't right. You're not taking time to be quiet and spend time with God.' I think God put her in my life to help me grow in Him."

From the beginning Bernie has consistently encouraged Carolyn to branch out creatively. "Bernie has always believed in me," she says gratefully. "From affirming my marriage to encouraging me as a mother, she has always expressed her belief in what I do. She was one of the first people to encourage me as an author." Bernie's constant encouragement and unwavering belief led to *Living the Questions: Making Sense of the Mess and Mystery of Life*, a funny, tender, and passionate collection of stories from Carolyn's life. "She was one of the first to get me thinking about writing it. All her encouragement and belief in me has made a big difference in my life."

Sometimes, believing in a friend can make all the difference in the world.

Carolyn currently chases her three-year-old son, Benjamin, around neighborhood parks in Vancouver, British Columbia, where she lives with her husband, Mark. She will soon be releasing her fifth studio album and is now writing her second book. Bernie works as a freelance writer in Nashville and is completing her third book.

How rare and wonderful
is that flash of a moment
when we realize we have
discovered a friend.

WILLIAM E. ROTHSCHILD

MAC &
AIMEE POWELL

God created no closer relationship outside of one with Him than that of husband and wife. If God is kept at the center of our marriages, there will be no one who encourages, challenges, inspires, motivates, or believes in us like our spouses. They're the ones who give us the confidence we need to spread our wings in a leap of faith, the ones who pick us up when we fail miserably, and the ones who strengthen and support us when we get up off the floor to try again. On this side of heaven we will experience no greater love than that of a God-centered husband or wife. Mac Powell is quick to name his wife, Aimee, as this kind of love. More than that, she's his best friend. "I really don't have a friend closer than her," he says with tremendous devotion.

Mac was a self-confessed geek in high school. The tall, skinny youth sported then what he thought was a cool haircut—short in front, long and ratty in the back. "It was hideous," the Third Day lead singer blurts. "If that wasn't bad enough, I had one of those mustaches that's barely there—it looked like dirt on my upper lip. It was a scumstache!" Mac heartily laughs at the visual image of himself. "It's a wonder anyone was friends with me, let alone somebody as cute and pretty as Aimee."

Aimee and Mac became acquainted in band. He played the trumpet and couldn't help but notice how striking Aimee looked marching in parades playing the piccolo—her long, red, straight hair beautifully cascading down her shoulders and back. "I was drawn to her because of that beautiful red hair," Mac affectionately recalls. "She was one of those people who was so genuine. She was such a nice, sweet girl." Through conversations at band practice, Mac soon learned that Aimee was a Christian.

"I'd accepted the Lord as Savior when I was younger," reflects Mac, "but God was never really real to me. He was never important enough to have a close relationship with. I never really understood or took the time to under-stand the full extent of my Christianity and what it meant; but then I met Aimee, and she played a huge role in bringing me closer to the Lord."

There was a quality in Aimee's personality and demeanor that spoke to Mac's heart. "I believed her genuineness," he says. "She wasn't like other Christians who said they were Christians but whose lives didn't reflect their words. She said she was a Christian, and she was totally genuine in her faith. She loved me as a Christian sister would. She would always encourage me, witness to me, and ask me to church." Mac finally relented and went to church with the persistent Aimee. "Of course it wasn't too hard to go and sit next to a pretty girl," he laughs.

What started out as a band-buddies friendship—talking, laughing, and going to church together—soon turned to romance at the end of Mac's senior and Aimee's junior year. Perhaps it was because Mac was the "Big Man in Band"—he had the coveted role of drum major. "I was the big geek who waved the stick in the air at the head of all parades," he says laughing. "Man, I was something!" They began to test the waters to see if their relationship would be able to evolve into one of a deeper love. "That was scary," Mac states. "You never know if it's going to work out, and if it doesn't, if it's going to ruin the friendship. We started dating, although I wasn't totally committed to the Lord at that time."

MAC POWELL OF THIRD DAY
WITH WIFE, AIMEE, &
DAUGHTER, SCOUT

They dated for two years but eventually decided it would be best if they broke up. "For the next two years, we didn't date," states Mac, "and in that time God prepared our hearts for one another in ways we could never have imagined." Mac finally asked Aimee to be his wife, and since their wedding in 1996, the two have only grown closer. "The Lord has blessed my life with such an influential friend," Mac says overwhelmed. "I have no better friend in this world, and there's no one I've ever met who is quite like her. Not even close. She's such a loving person—she reached out to me in high school with absolute and total love, but at the same time she's sassy. There's not a lot of gray in Aimee's life. Something is either black or white. She wants people to be the best that they can be and to choose the right path for their lives."

From the moment they met, Aimee has encouraged Mac to be the best at anything he tried: from writing to singing to his walk with God. "The first year of my ministry was hard on us," Mac recalls. "It's hard on anybody that first year out—and it's still hard—but Aimee's *always* encouraged me to stay focused on the ministry. It's so much more than just music and making a living to her." Times of loneliness still overtake the couple when Mac's on the road, but the two have resolved to cover one another in prayer during those long stretches. "We'd talk on the phone, and sometimes she'd cry about something and I'd hate that I couldn't be there with her. It really started tearing both of us apart, and we realized Satan would use those times we were away from each other to drive a wedge between us, to try to tear apart the ministry. When you're in ministry, life can be kind of crazy, but Aimee does an awesome job at handling me, the baby, and continuing to grow in her own walk with the Lord."

> IT SHOULD BE BASED ON AGAPE LOVE. FRIENDSHIP IS A LOVE FOR ANOTHER PERSON THAT IS NOT SELF-SATISFYING BUT SACRIFICIAL AND UNCONDITIONAL.
>
> MAC POWELL

The "baby" is Mac and Aimee's little girl, Scout, whom they joyfully welcomed in July of 1999. Mac's great love, adoration, and respect for his wife only deepened after Scout's arrival. "It is *amazing* to see the mother she is," he says in heartfelt awe. "The incredible love she has as a mother just blows me away, and it breaks my heart to see it. My heart literally wants to burst from the love I have for her when I watch her with the baby. It's incredible."

Late one evening as Mac worked tirelessly on writing new songs for an upcoming album, Aimee indicated that she was going to bed. Mac said good night and continued to work on a song. "Aren't you coming?" Aimee asked. He noted that he was right in the middle of a song and would like to finish it before the ideas left him. Aimee wearily trudged to bed alone, kissing Scout before falling asleep herself. Around one in the morning, a half-asleep Aimee stumbled from the dark bedroom into the well-lit room where Mac was working. Squinting through the bright lights she said, "I love you and I love your music—the songs you write. And I don't want to do anything to ever discourage you and your writing, so spend as much time as you need," and fumbled her way back to bed.

"That's what love is," Mac exclaims. "It's sacrificial. What Aimee does reminds me of the verse in John 15 that states, 'Greater love has no one than this, that he lay down his life for his friends.' Aimee lays down her life as a sacrifice. She frequently sacrifices her own desires for the sake of the ministry—and all those little sacrifices add up. She is a friend who constantly lays aside her own plans and lays aside her life for her friends. She is the greatest friend I've ever had!"

Third Day has recently released their fourth album. Mac and Aimee continue to learn more about their faith and relationship with God as they raise Scout in a suburb north of Atlanta.

To the query, "What is a friend?"
his reply was "A single soul
dwelling in two bodies."

ARISTOTLE

a single
soul

dwelling
in two bodies

LIFT US UP

BEFORE THE
KING OF KINGS

friendship

We all need sheltering trees

Friends in our lives

who'll get down on their knees

And lift us up before

the King of Kings

We all need sheltering trees

MARK WILLS & CHARLES WILKES

*S*ometimes a friend has been a part of the landscape of your life for so long that it's difficult to pinpoint the day you met or the circumstances that brought you together. All you know is that he or she has always been there as a stable companion, a solid comrade, a constant friend. A friend who doesn't change with the level of your personal status or income. A friend who doesn't require conversation in order to be comfortable. A friend who knows everything there is to know about you and chooses to hang out with you anyway.

Long before he was an established voice on country radio, multiplatinum-selling artist Mark Wills found such a friend in Charles Wilkes. "I didn't know it then, but that guy was going to be a constant force in my life," says the affable, down-to-earth singer.

Charles had just been transferred to Atlanta from Nashville and had a family of his own when he met the Wills family in church. As a boy of ten, Mark would rather hang with his buddies than his parents' friends, but there was something about Charles's childlike qualities that always captured his attention. "He's a jokester," claims Mark. "He's always been real aggressive but in a funny way. He makes me laugh. That's just part of his personality. People feel pretty much at ease around him." Even at his young age, Mark was already interested in music, which drew him even closer to the musically inclined Charles. "He has a real natural ability for singing," Mark states. "He'd sing in church, and I remember thinking, *Man, that guy can sing*. He'd direct the singing at church sometimes, and he always had so much fun doing it. I was too young to really know it then, but we had a lot of similar traits in our personalities."

Both men share the same witty sense of humor, don't take themselves too seriously, and have a deep love for family and a great appreciation for the perfect practical joke. "He loves to laugh," Mark chuckles, describing the congenial fifty-year-old Charles. "I think that's why we've been friends for so long—because we both have a sense of humor about life. If you hang around Charles for any length of time, you have to!"

As a young boy, Mark was a tremendous fan of the country group Alabama. "I'm still a huge fan," he says admiringly. One day when the aspiring country superstar was thirteen years old, he answered the phone and the voice on the other end immediately asked whom he was talking to.

"This is Mark," he answered, somewhat bored.

"Hey, Mark," the voice replied. "This is Randy Owen."

Instantly recognizing the name of Alabama's front man and lead singer, Mark's mind raced for the right words to say to his idol.

"Hey! How you doing?" he asked in an attempt to sound cool yet not overly excited.

"I'm good. Real good. I heard you were a big Alabama fan?"

NO MATTER WHO YOU ARE, WHAT COLOR YOU ARE, OR ANYTHING ELSE— A FRIEND BELIEVES IN YOU AND TRUSTS IN YOU.

MARK WILLS

Mark's heart raced with the anticipation of what would come next. "Yeah, I love you guys," he exclaimed.

"Well, we're over here in Ft. Payne, and I thought I'd call and see if you want to come over to the house."

Mark couldn't be sure, but he was almost certain his heart had stopped beating, rendering him speechless.

"Mark," the voice continued. "Is your dad around so I can talk to him?"

"Yeah," Mark finally uttered. Racing at Olympic speed, he found his father and pulled him to the phone, joyously repeating words he had only dreamed of saying one day, "Randy Owen's on the phone. He wants *me* to come over to his house!"

Picking up the phone, Mark's dad burst into laughter nearly from the word *hello*. Mark anxiously waited to hear what his country idol was sharing with his dad. His father was still laughing when he hung up the receiver. "What'd he say?" Mark eagerly asked.

"That was *Charles Wilkes*," his father laughed.

His dream of sharing barbecued ribs with Randy Owen obliterated, Mark laughed along with his father at the practical joke that had just been pulled at his expense. "There wasn't anything to do but laugh," he says, jovially recalling the memory. "That's why I like Charles. He laughs at himself and makes me sit back and laugh at myself."

In 1999 at the annual Fan Fair event in Nashville, which attracts thousands of country fans around the country, Mark was asked to play in the annual City of Hope celebrity softball tournament. The charity match pits one team of country artists against another as thousands of fans cheer and scream from the stands. Mark was playing third base when Dean Sams from the group Lonestar screamed a ball his way. "It was going straight for the head of the Nashville Predators hockey coach," Mark says dramatically, "so I reached out to catch the ball right when he flung his arm and accidentally knocked my glove away." The ball thumped Mark's eye with a resounding thud. "It split my eye wide open," he says proudly.

MARK WILLS & CHARLES WILKES

Following the game, Charles drove to a nearby Wal-Mart, bought a child's baseball glove, and took it to the paint department. The sales associates raised only a few eyebrows as they painted the mitt gold and handed it back to their mischievous customer. That evening as the swollen, black-eyed Mark greeted fans at the fan-club party in his honor, Charles stopped the activity to present Mark with The Gold Glove Award for Outstanding Fielder. "That's just how his mind works," he says laughing. "As if it wasn't embarrassing enough getting hit in front of everybody, then he has to remind me of it all over again!"

But that's what constant friends do—in their own gentle, loving, funny way, they remind us of who we are and where we've come from. They help us look at ourselves for who we really are, not who people think we are. "He doesn't care that I'm a singer," Mark states. "He doesn't care how many number one songs I chart or how many gold or platinum records I sell. He's always known me for Mark, and that's just the way it is with him—I'm the same guy he met when he

SHELTERING TREES

moved to Atlanta. And when he talks to me, it's never him talking to some country singer; he's just talking to that kid he watched grow up."

After many days on the road, Mark looks forward to just spending time
at home, "not doing anything in particular," which might include just driving
around with no particular place to go with Charles. "We don't have to do anything together," he says easily. "We can ride around all day and never talk
about anything, but it's fun for both of us. That's a good time."

Charles's son and daughter are just a few years younger than Mark himself, but the age difference has never dampened their friendship. "He's like
another dad," he explains. "He's someone I can call and ask for advice, and I
know it's going to be good because he's got some years of wisdom behind
him. He's a great friend to turn to. I have a lot of friends, but we don't share
the many years I share with Charles. To have somebody like Charles who's
known me for so long, who's been there for so long, has made a real impact
on me. He's been a good, good friend for a whole lot of years and has never
asked for anything other than friendship in return. That's it."

And that's just what a constant friend does best.

*Mark has released one gold and two double platinum coun-
try albums. In 1999, he was voted Top New Male Vocalist by the Academy of
Country Music. He has charted several number one hits including "I Do Cherish You,"
"Don't Laugh at Me," and "Wish You Were Here." He lives with his wife, Kelly, and
daughter, Mally, in Georgia. Charles works as a salesman/supervisor for a construction
company in the Atlanta area. He and his wife, Charlotte, have two grown children.*

100

A friend is one who

walks in when the rest

of the world walks out.

WALTER WINCHELL

MICHELLE MCKINNEY HAMMOND & BRENDA BLONSKI

Michelle McKinney Hammond loves to laugh. She loves to approach each day with the attitude of, "Lord, what are we going to do today?" and then jump in with both feet. She sees life as an amazing gift wrapped with incredible blessings, joys, and grace. One of her friends termed having a great day as a Michelle McKinney Hammond Day. But in 1979, long before she was having a Michelle McKinney Hammond Day, the popular author and speaker was walking on the wild side in Chicago. She was loud, brash, and bordering on obnoxious. She loved dancing the night away and savoring a good smoke. She had an uncanny knack for finding the best parties and rubbing shoulders with the rich and famous. Many of her coworkers at the advertising agency where she worked didn't approve of Michelle's lusty approach to life. "Brenda Blonski and Michelle Taylor would try to sneak out of the office for lunch without letting me know," she giggles. "Michelle put up with me because we had to share an office, but Brenda just flat out did not like me!" Even though she and Brenda also happened to be neighbors, the two never socialized. "We never did anything together because she didn't like me," she says through roars of laughter.

After a particularly exciting day at work, Michelle went home, euphoric and dancing on cloud nine. Soon after arriving home for the evening, she was jolted with the news that her boyfriend, who had gone on a vacation to California, had been shot and killed. "I was in shock," she says steadily. "I thought, *Who do I call? I need to call somebody*." Michelle quickly called her neighbor Brenda and asked if she would come over. "Brenda then turned around and called Michelle to go with her," she cackles with laughter. "She didn't want to be stuck with me alone!" The women arrived and simply sat with Michelle. "They didn't say much," she remembers fondly. "They didn't know what to say, but it meant a lot to me that they were there. They were just *there* and listened as I cried and went on."

Shortly after her boyfriend's death, Michelle gave what scraps there were left of her life to God. "I'd lived my life my way long enough," she exclaims. Excited and energized by her new lifestyle, Michelle eagerly shared her life-changing experience with Brenda. "She wouldn't have any of it," she chuckles. "She'd been put off by me so many times that she wasn't the least bit interested in listening to me." Viewing Brenda as more than just a tough nut to crack, Michelle rolled up her sleeves and got down to serious soul-winning business. "I went on a seven-day fast for that girl, and by the time it was over, I was taking her to heaven with me," Michelle explodes in shrieks of laughter. But sad times were ahead.

Brenda's father died, leaving her mother alone and scared. "Brenda called me and said her mom was afraid to be by herself, so I volunteered to go stay with her and help her with things." From that time on, a secure bond was formed between them. The women decided to move in together, and they encouraged each other daily, reading and studying Scripture together, praying together, holding each other accountable. "From the moment she knew the Lord, she has been nothing but consistent in her faith," Michelle says of her friend, amazed. "Her consistency has always given me something to reach for in my own life."

Nearly six months after the women became roommates, Michelle moved to California to pursue a love interest and what she hoped would be a brand-new start. During that time Brenda became engaged. "I was somewhat opposed to her marrying this guy," Michelle recalls. "Looking back on it, I know I must have hurt her deeply with the things I said. I talked to her one day, and she said, 'Michelle, I've heard everything you have to say, and I'm going to pray and ask God what I should do.' I sure am glad she had the sense to ignore me that time. She is a woman of prayer! Her attitude is always, 'I have to give this to the Lord.' Well she prayed and she prayed and she prayed and she called one day and said, 'Michelle, I've prayed about this, and I feel he's the man God wants me to marry, and I don't want to live without him!' There is a great depth to Brenda. She communicates with God, and *then* she speaks. She has a sense of knowing when to quiet her spirit and really listen to people. She's challenged me in my own life to just be quiet and listen. She reminds me of the Holy Spirit. You cannot be obnoxious around Brenda because she has such a compassionate, quiet center about her."

Finding her "love interest" in California not so interesting after all,

Michelle moved back to Chicago and became involved in a serious relationship that appeared to be heading for the altar of her dreams. "I thought for sure he was the man I would marry." Working in her office one afternoon, Michelle received a phone call from her boyfriend saying he was marrying another woman. In shock, she hung up the phone and sat paralyzed in her chair. "I couldn't cry I was so stunned," she says, recalling the pain. "I couldn't even move. I couldn't move any part of my body." When Brenda discovered her in this catatonic condition, Michelle weakly let the news tumble from her lips. Brenda wrapped her arms around her broken friend and sobbed, crying the tears of pain and rejection that Michelle was unable to cry herself. "She felt my pain in such a real way that her tears prompted me to release my own. She never said a word to me. She just held on to me and cried. She shared the burden of my loss and took on the pain of my hurt in a way that reminded me so much of Jesus. She is the picture of what a Christian should be."

Michelle and Brenda both had a mutual burden for Michelle Taylor to know God's love in a personal way. "We tag-teamed her," Michelle says, laughing. "I was like John the Baptist, and Brenda was very sweet and kind like Jesus. It was exciting to work together for God. Before long, Michelle gave her life to the Lord, more through Brenda's influence than mine. I was probably the reason it took so long; I was so heavy-handed. When I first became a Christian, I prayed that God would give me *some* real friends, and he has blessed me exceedingly and abundantly above what I could ask or think. Brenda, Michelle, and another dear friend, Theresa Hayden, have been a part

> ALL MY FRIENDS HAVE SHOWN ME THE LOVE OF GOD.
>
> MICHELLE MCKINNEY HAMMOND

105

of my Christian walk almost from the very beginning, and the core between us has never been broken. We made a decision to walk in covenant together. We've confronted each other with some tough issues. It's hard to take and give correction, but we do it out of love for one another. That's what friends have to do."

With active lives and schedules, the close-knit group of friends don't see each other as much as they'd like, although they have four appointments they're diligent to keep each year. "Our birthdays are the time we get together for dinner and a time of prayer and blessing for the birthday girl. We actually tape-record the prayers and blessings and review them over the year to see how God has answered us. Things always happen when we pray together." The friends perform what Michelle calls, "active maintenance of the friendship. We hold each other accountable," she says. "We all feel that friendship begins and ends with God; He is the core, and that makes all the difference in the world. But none of that means maintaining a friendship is easy. Keeping God at the center makes it *easier*, but it's still hard work. When you go into a friendship, you have to realize that there's going to be work involved in an ongoing friendship—but it's worth it. I've seen the rewards!"

With friends like that, every day is a Michelle McKinney Hammond Day!

Michelle speaks throughout the country and is the author of such books as What to Do Until Love Finds You *and* The Power of Femininity. *She will soon be releasing her tenth book,* How to Be Blessed and Highly Favored. *Brenda has worked more than twenty years at the same ad agency but is transitioning into full-time ministry with her husband, Bill, a pastor. They have two children, Adam and Alexanna.*

MICHELLE MCKINNEY HAMMOND
& BRENDA BLONSKI

You can face the highest mountain

and the climb won't feel so high

Or cross the darkest valley

and it won't seem so wide

Nothing is impossible

when a friend is by your side

NOTHING
IS IMPOSSIBLE

WHEN A FRIEND
IS BY YOUR SIDE

Friendship

REBECCA LYNN HOWARD,
SHANNON WHITE,
JOSH WHITAKER,
JIMMY HOWARD

On Rebecca Lynn Howard's eighteenth birthday, she signed a recording contract with a Nashville country record label—not a bad gift for someone who'd left eastern Kentucky only a few months earlier with dreams of becoming country music's next female vocalist of the year. That same year she was asked to sing on the soundtrack for *The Apostle*, starring Robert Duvall, winning a Grammy award. Through her publishing deal, the accomplished young songwriter would soon hear her songs cut on albums by John Michael Montgomery, Patty Loveless, and her idol, Reba McIntire. But the successes of her career have had little effect on the now twenty-one-year-old. "Sometimes things happen in life that put everything into perspective," she says in a voice that belies her tender years.

During Rebecca Lynn's last quarter of high school, she moved to Nashville to pursue her dream of a career in country music. "My friends Josh, Shannon, and Jimmy were my biggest cheerleaders," she affectionately remembers. "I'd known Josh Whitaker since elementary school, and we were just the biggest buddies. He'd always make me sing for him," she laughs. When Rebecca's and Josh's elementary school joined other local schools in junior high, they met Shannon White and Jimmy Howard. "We all became instant friends," she fondly recalls. The good-natured boys possessed an undeniable zest for life and saw the humorous side of any situation. "They were crackerjacks," she exclaims. "All three of them were cutups. They loved to laugh; they loved to make people laugh. They were all huge pranksters. All of them had that same quality," she says softly, "that same sweet, funny quality. I enjoy people like that as friends—people who can laugh at themselves and make other people laugh. That's a wonderful quality to have in life."

In February of 1997, shortly after Rebecca's move to Nashville, she received a call from Shannon's fiancée, asking her to sing at their wedding. Rebecca couldn't think of a better way to honor her dear friend than to participate in the most exciting day of his life. Tears rimmed her eyes as she watched her friend say his vows, as memories of their laughing and joking together in school ran through her mind. "It was a great day," she recalls. "He was so happy." The two-o'clock wedding took place on a Saturday. Exactly five days later at two o'clock, the phone rang in Nashville. Rebecca stood in silence as the voice on the other end asked if she would sing at Shannon's funeral. A car accident had suddenly ended his young life. "I couldn't do it," she remembers. "It was just too hard to face the fact of singing at his funeral when I had just sung at his wedding. I didn't have the strength to do it."

Writing songs was the cathartic release Rebecca used to deal with the enormous loss of her friend. "I really dove into writing because it was just too painful to think of his entire life ahead of him and how it was gone. I know things happen for a reason and that there's a plan for everything, but that doesn't necessarily make the loss any less painful."

Nearly five months after Shannon's death, Rebecca received another devastating phone call from her hometown of Salyersville, Kentucky. Josh had somehow lost control of his vehicle, crashed, and instantly died. Jimmy traveled from college to act as a pallbearer at his friend's funeral. "Jimmy and I talked. We were reliving the good, sweet times in school, talking about how much both Josh and Shannon meant to us. It was so hard to believe they were gone. It didn't seem possible." Later that night, before leaving for Nashville, Rebecca went out to eat with her family. Someone entered the restaurant who knew Rebecca and relayed the tragic news that Jimmy had fallen asleep at the wheel and was killed on his way back to college. "I didn't know what to do. I didn't know how it could all be possible." The beautiful rolling green hills that were the backdrop of so much joy and happiness during Rebecca's youth had somehow claimed the lives of all three of her friends.

"It's hard to look at sixteen-to-eighteen-year-olds in a coffin," she states. "You never expect that your friendships will end that way. You assume that life will separate you as you get older and start a family of your own, but you don't think their lives will end tragically. In six months' time I lost three of my dearest friends in the whole world. They were all such wonderful friends. People need to be aware that friendships don't just end by people growing apart; sometimes they end abruptly—and that's heart-wrenching."

After Josh's and Jimmy's funerals, Rebecca asked her manager to keep her busy; busyness would help keep her mind from dwelling on the tragic sorrow of the previous six months. "But eventually my schedule slowed down, and I was faced with the reality of their deaths," she explains. "I sat in my apartment and had a genuine cry party. I let it all out in big gushes, and it was at that moment that a song came to my mind. I poured every emotion into that song, and then peace came over me. It was God's way of comforting me and helping me with the loss." The song "I Took You for Granted" is a tender tribute to Shannon, Josh, and Jimmy. In it she wrote, "You would always be there, when I needed you to talk to. Now a part of me is gone; it died along there with you."

> IT'S BRUTALLY HONEST— THAT'S THE BIGGEST PART OF A FRIENDSHIP. AND IF IT'S A TRUE FRIENDSHIP, YOU'LL GET OVER THE BRUTAL PART.
>
> REBECCA LYNN HOWARD

Rebecca doesn't dwell on the sadness or the what-might-have-been aspect of each of her friend's lives. "You look for answers, but there aren't any," she offers somberly, her sweet southern voice slightly trailing off. "There will never be any answers here on earth. All I can do is reflect on the good things about their lives. I visit their grave sites and know they're not there. They're in a much better place. I don't worry about what would have been, because I know where they are now and that they're happy. There are different levels of friendships, but the four of us had a genuine, open friendship with one another. That's the purest form of friendship. They were true friends in every sense of the word. They would do anything for anybody but especially for their friends. That's what true friendship is all about: going out of your way for a friend."

A community of friends poured into church for each boy's funeral; the overflow of mourners stood on the sidewalk craning their necks to hear the services. "That's how loved they were," Rebecca states emphatically. "They were friends to so many others, and everyone came out to honor them."

Since the tragedies of 1997, Rebecca holds friendships closer than ever. "I've always cherished my friends," she says slowly, "but I cherish them more than ever now. I don't hold anything back. If I want to say I love them, I tell them. I don't put it off until the next time I see them, because I know there might not be a next time."

With each fall, Rebecca reflects on the short yet poignant lives of her friends. "They all died right around this time," she offers, "but ironically, fall is my favorite time of year. A lot of people see fall as death, but I see it as their birth in heaven, and that gives me peace. I'm sad that our friendships ended the way they did, but on the bigger scale, they didn't. I know we'll always be friends and that when I see them again, our friendship will continue."

Rebecca continues to write for other artists and has just finished her second country album. She has opened for Vince Gill, Patty Loveless, Willie Nelson, Kenny Rogers, and Brad Paisley. Her powerhouse vocals have been heard on albums by Dolly Parton and others. She has been married for two years and lives with her husband, Jason, in Nashville.

I count myself in nothing

else so happy

As in a soul remembering

my good friends.

WILLIAM SHAKESPEARE

ZIG ZIGLAR & DR. DWIGHT "IKE" REIGHARD

There is a stigma, a code of honor, that has surrounded men for centuries. It is a code that says it's manly for men to talk about sports, cars, and women but that it's unmanly—even unacceptable—to talk about feelings, emotions, and struggles. An invisible sign is posted on the door of every male locker room in America that reads, "No intimate feelings allowed." *Intimacy* is for the female gender only. Throughout the ages, from father to son, brother to brother, and friend to friend, men have knowingly and willingly kept expressions of intimacy or talk of real feelings out of their male relationships. Real men don't want and don't *need* such nonsense mucking up their conversations.

One of America's top motivational speakers and internationally recognized author Zig Ziglar and his friend Dr. Dwight "Ike" Reighard began to shatter that myth almost from the moment they met. "We bonded from the beginning," Zig claims. "We're birds of a feather, really." In 1985, while Ike was guest-preaching at a church in Dallas on overcoming giants in your life, he quoted from the Zig Ziglar book *See You at the Top*. "I read that book, and it changed my life," Ike says. "I always encouraged people to read it and would often quote from it, like I did that Sunday morning." At the end of the service a tall, thin, immaculately dressed man approached Ike and said, "I really like what you had to say about Zig Ziglar." Ike replied, "Oh, are you a Zig fan?" The "fan" paused for just a moment before saying, "I am Zig!" Ike couldn't believe it. "That's pretty dumb, isn't it?" he laughs. "What an idiot I was. Here I was saying how much I admired Zig, and I couldn't even recognize the man when he's standing right in front of me!"

The two men discovered that they had both come from poor child-hoods. "We came from hard backgrounds," Zig offers. Zig's father had died when he was a boy of five, leaving his mother to raise six children who were too young to work during the Depression. Ike grew up with parents who loved and cared for him tremendously, but the young boy never had any personal motivation toward achievement or accomplishment in life. "My mother and father had only a fifth-grade education," he states, "and my father worked in a rock quarry most of his life." They were wonderful parents but didn't know how to challenge him to strive for any particular goals. He says, "With my academic acumen, it was an achievement just to get out of high school!"

But there was something in young Ike that knew he had to dream dreams that would take him beyond the borders of Atlanta. He worked as a disc jockey before deciding to enter college; but with no motivation to succeed, he failed his courses and was thrown out of school. Then Ike picked up a copy of Zig's *See You at the Top* and began writing down his goals, putting college graduation at the top of the list. "He went back and literally cried his way back in," Zig laughs. "That's how important it was for him to finish. The school put him on probation, and two and a half years later, he graduated cum laude and went on to earn his doctorate!"

As the two new friends finished talking in the corridors of the First Baptist Church, Ike asked Zig to mentor him; and for the next several years, Zig graciously poured much of what he had learned in life into the eager Ike. "When you mentor someone, you make an incredible investment of time into that person's life," says Ike. "Zig made an invaluable investment into my life through his teaching and availability."

Two years before he met Zig, Ike lost both his wife of twelve years and what would have been their firstborn child during childbirth. A mere ten years after they met, Ike would share what he had learned in his tunnel of grief to help Zig through his own. In 1995 Zig's oldest child, Suzan, a devoted wife and mother of two daughters, died three days after her forty-sixth birthday from pulmonary fibrosis, a lung condition that can be fatal unless the patient receives a lung transplant. As doctors delivered the news that there was only a short time left in Suzan's life, Zig and his entire family gathered around her bed. Passages from the Psalms were read and a hymn was sung—a pastor's lone voice filling the room as God's presence enveloped them all. Surrounded by those who loved her most on earth, Suzan quietly stepped into the arms of the One who loved her most of all. After the medical tubes and machines were disconnected from Suzan's body, the family gathered closely one more time around her bed and joined hands in prayer. Then they each kissed her good-bye.

After Suzan's death, the man whom Ike calls "the most positive person I've ever met" spiraled in his grief. "There is no hurt equal to that of losing a child," Zig says solemnly. "It's the most unnatural thing a person will ever face. There were twelve in my family; only three of us are living now. I have buried my parents, my brothers and sisters—but there is *nothing* close to the grief you feel at the loss of a child."

When death claims someone we love, we are often left numb: Our prayers are paralyzed, our dreams deci- mated. Zig, who for years had motivated millions to see their dreams through to reality, sought the comfort and

> HE'S TAUGHT ME HOW TO DREAM; BUT EVEN MORE THAN THAT, HE'S TAUGHT ME HOW TO TURN THOSE DREAMS INTO REALITY. IF YOU FIND A FRIEND WHO CAN DO THAT, YOU'LL HAVE FOUND THE GREATEST FRIEND IN THE WORLD.
>
> IKE REIGHARD

encouragement of friends to help him out of his own long tunnel of grief, to help him *want* to dream again. "Zig would ask me how to channel his grief," Ike recalls. "He never thought of himself only as the guy who was teaching me something—he genuinely sought my counsel, learning from me and others how to overcome his grief. He has so much knowledge and discern- ment in things. He's like the consummate big brother that you can gain wis- dom from, but he's never too proud to seek wisdom from others."

Regarding the wisdom of God, Charles Haddon Spurgeon once said, "God is too good to be unkind, God is too wise to be mistaken, so when you can't trace His hand, trust His heart." Reflecting on the pain and grief he felt after the loss of his wife and child, Ike was quick to share this quote of com- fort and others like it that helped him with his grieving friend. "He was always ready, willing, and anxious to give me help and encouragement at that time," remembers Zig. "Ike would give me support and Scripture references to reflect on. He would drop notes to me, call me—I'm fortunate to have a friend like Ike whom I can depend on in times like that. Proverbs 17:17 says, 'A friend is always loyal and a brother is born to help in time of need.' Ike is the personification of loyalty. And as far as our relationship is concerned, Proverbs 27:9 sums it up quite well: 'The heartfelt counsel of a friend is as sweet perfume and incense.' And Ike does give heartfelt, wise counsel."

Men, who in general aren't as comfortable comforting one another as women are, often suffer the most through pain of any sort. They stuff their hurts, swallow their grief, and hide their suffering, often lashing out in retaliation against society as a whole. "Bill Glass has been in more than 350 prisons across this country," Zig offers. "In his ministry he has never found a man in prison who genuinely loved his father or had a strong relationship with him. Out of the forty thousand people incarcerated in the state of Florida, 94 percent of them are men—only thirteen of them are Jewish men. Out of the seventy-five hundred imprisoned in Arkansas, only seven of them are Jewish. In one three-year study of thirty-six thousand men incarcerated in the navy and marines, only three of the thirty-six thousand were Jewish." It is customary within the Jewish faith for a father to greet his son with an embrace saying, "Bless you, my son. I love you, my son," followed by a kiss—words and actions of affirmation. This is true whether the son is three years old or fifty years old. "I believe that men today are more intimate with one another than they were twenty years ago," Zig claims. "They're more receptive to that now than they were in the past. That holds true in my own life. My son is thirty-five, and he's far more my son now than he was as a child. Now, whenever I see my son, I hug him. I haven't always done that, and it made an already marvelous relationship even better. That's growing."

For the past sixteen years, Zig has happily grown alongside his friend Ike, admiring his great faith and encouraging spirit. "Ike has impacted my life primarily as an encourager. He has tremendous biblical knowledge and insight. He puts his whole heart and soul in what he does—in helping people change their lives through faith. Behind his bubbling, gregarious personality is a man with a purpose!"

Ike points to Zig's genuine positive attitude as an identifying mark of his friendship. "He doesn't have a Pollyanna positiveness but a genuinely positive outlook that comes from his walk with God," Ike says. "He'll be the first to tell you that it's the most important relationship in his life. As Billy Graham is the clergyman known for integrity, I think Zig is *the* businessman known for integrity. I attribute so much of what I've experienced to his positive influence. First through his books and then through his friendship, he made me feel that my life could have worth and that I could actually accomplish something." In his best-selling book *Over the Top*, Zig claims Ike went from being "a wandering generality to a meaningful specific." "I did that through Zig's help," Ike says gratefully. "I did that through the investment he made in my life. That's what a friend does. He's someone who makes an investment in your life and grows along with you, helping you to grow. If I had to give one definition of a best friend, it's the person who brings out the very best in you. Zig has been that friend to me."

121

Zig sums up friendship this way: "If you go out in life looking for friends, they'll be difficult to find. If you go out in life to be a friend, you'll find them everywhere. Ike goes out to be friend, so he has them everywhere."

Embracing one another in pain, sharing their burdens, and encouraging each other in the faith have helped Zig and Ike shatter the macho stigma associated with male relationships. "You have to have access into a man's life," Ike offers. "If there's ever going to be any real growing, he has to allow you into his feelings and emotions, and you have to allow access into your life as well."

And that's just what Zig and Ike have done—not because they're weak or unmanly but because that's what real men do.

Zig is the best-selling author of more than seventeen books and one of the top motivational speakers in the country. He lives with "The Redhead," his wife of fifty-four years, in Dallas. Ike is the senior pastor of North Star Church in Kennesaw, Georgia. He has written two books, travels as an affirmational speaker, and serves on the board of several corporations and universities. "Pretty good for a guy who had no education," he laughs.

Winning has always
meant much to me, but winning
friends has meant the most.

friends meant the most

BABE DIDRIKSON ZAHARIAS

WE ALL
NEED
SHELTERING
TREES

friendship

We all need sheltering trees

Friends in our lives

who'll get down on their knees

And lift us up before

the King of Kings

We all need sheltering trees

If you live to be a hundred,

I want to live to be a hundred

minus one day, so I never have

to live without you.

⁓

WINNIE THE POOH

From singable, energetic songs to gripping, lyric-based ballads, NewSong's power-pop music is their entry into evangelism. Their life-changing concerts as well as sixteen #1 radio singles and numerous Dove award nominations are signs of their continuous impact on people's lives. This, their latest CD, features the #1 pop holiday smash "The Christmas Shoes."